THE
SHADOW
OF THE
APOCALYPSE

THE
SHADOW
OF THE
APOCALYPSE

WHEN ALL HELL BREAKS LOOSE

PAUL CROUCH

G. P. PUTNAM'S SONS

NEW YORK

While the author has made every effort to provide accurate telephone
numbers and Internet addresses at the time of publication, neither
the publisher nor the author assumes any responsibility for errors,
or for changes that occur after publication.

ıllP

G. P. Putnam's Sons
Publishers Since 1838
a member of
Penguin Group (USA) Inc.
375 Hudson Street
New York, NY 10014

All scriptural quotations from King James Version unless
otherwise indicated.

Scriptural quotations in Foreword from the New American Standard Bible,
Copyright © 1960, 1962, 1963, 1968, 1971, 1972, 1973, 1975, 1977, 1995
by The Lockman Foundation
Used by permission. (www.Lockman.org)

Bible codes used on pages 22 and 25 are from *The Bible Code*
by Michael Drosnin (Simon & Schuster, 1977).
Bible codes used on pages 29, 71, 81, 82 and 112 courtesy
of Yacov Rambsel.
All art on page 189 from *September 11 Is in the Bible Code*
by Dr. Larry Mitcham (Pacific International University, 2001).

Library of Congress Cataloging-in-Publication Data

Crouch, Paul F.
The shadow of the apocalypse : when all hell breaks loose / Paul Crouch.
p.   cm.
ISBN 0-399-14941-4
1. Bible—Prophecies.   I. Title.
BS647.3C76   2004   2003063250
236'.9—dc22

Printed in the United States of America
1   3   5   7   9   10   8   6   4   2

This book is printed on acid-free paper. ∞

This book is dedicated to the writers of the sacred Scriptures: the prophet Daniel and the apostle John, whose prophetic visions made this entire book posible, and to the faithful Holy Spirit who inspired them.

Acknowledgments

My special thanks go to Yacov Rambsel, whose invaluable research into the Bible codes provided the foundation and framework for this book. Also, my thanks and appreciation to Linda Holland, who helped take complicated concepts and explain them in layman's language; Karen Scalf Linamen for her editorial assistance; and Russell Willett for his expertise. I'd also like to thank my faithful assistant, Margie Tuccillo, for all her efforts with this project.

Thank you, Denise Silvestro, for your insights and creativity; Joel Fotinos, for your enthusiasm, encouragement, and wisdom; and to everyone at Putnam. My gratitude to Susan Petersen Kennedy, Marilyn Ducksworth, Michael Barson, Dan Harvey, Dick Heffernan, Chris Mosley, Martha Bushko, and everyone at JMS Marketing and Sales, Inc.

Contents

THE
SHADOW
OF THE
APOCALYPSE

Foreword

Hal Lindsey

I became a student of Bible prophecy forty-seven years ago due to an event that took place at Rice University. It was with a good deal of skepticism that I went there with a friend to hear a Rhodes scholar speak on the subject of "What the Bible Says about the Middle East Crisis." This referred to the raging crisis of that time, known as the Suez Crisis of 1956.

To my great surprise, I was astounded by the lecture. I never dreamed that there were clear predictions of precise events that would happen in concert shortly before the Second Coming of Jesus Christ. Many of these things concerned certain alignments of nations and conflicts in the Middle East. At the center was the predicted miraculous return of the Jews to reestablish the state of Israel. This had officially occurred on May 15, 1948.

That lecture launched me on a lifelong pursuit of seeking to understand Bible prophecy. It propelled me to go to graduate school and learn Greek and Hebrew in order to understand the original texts of the Bible. And this resulted in my writing many books on the subject, the first of which was *The Late Great Planet Earth.* I mention all of this to show my keen interest in the subject of Dr. Paul Crouch's book on Bible prophecy.

In 1973, I was invited for interview on a fledgling new television station by its founder, Paul Crouch. He and his wife, Jan, had just started this venture of faith and ambitiously called it the Trinity Broadcasting Network. I was immediately impressed by Paul's communicating skills, his understanding of Bible prophecy, and his great faith. We became friends in the years that followed. As Paul envisioned, TBN became the largest Christian television network in the world.

On many occasions, Dr. Crouch and I have discussed the key prophecy of the prophet Daniel. I believe this is a very important passage that shows how profoundly groundbreaking Dr. Crouch's new book is. Daniel received enormous predictions about the end times. However, he was puzzled by their meaning and pleaded with God to help him understand. This is the response God gave him: "Go your way, Daniel, for these words are concealed and sealed up until the end of time. Many will act wickedly, and none of the wicked will understand, but those who have insight will understand" (Daniel 12:8–10 NASB).

The two Hebrew verbs translated as *"concealed"* and *"sealed up"* in the passage above are actually from the same root Hebrew word, *SATAM.* Its first use is a command to "conceal the *words*" of the prophecies about the end times until near the time of their occurrence. The second time it is used is as a command but in a different verb stem. It commands Daniel to "seal up the *book* of prophecy" until near the end time.

In this context, the first command should be understood as *"encode"* or *"encrypt"* the *words* of prophecy until the end time." For about the last one hundred years the *book* of prophecy has been *"unsealed,"* but the *words* continued to be *"encrypted"* until very recently.

I believe that this new discovery of so-called Bible codes has initiated the search for the *encrypted* words of prophecy. In 1994, the prestigious *Journal of Statistical Sciences* published a paper regarding the newly announced "Equidistant Letter Sequence" or ELS theory, which proposed that by counting equal distances between letters in the original Hebrew Torah, certain words and phrases could be uncovered that bore an undeniable relationship to the surface text. For example, take Isaiah 53:10. The surface text paints a picture of the suffering Messiah, but by using ELS and counting from the yod (a Hebrew letter) and counting every twenty letters, we find *Yeshua shmi,* which means, "Yeshua is my name." And if we look at Zechariah 7:4 and from the first *yod* count every fifth letter from right to left, we will find *Yeshua.* In Leviticus 21:10, counting from *heh* counting every third letter from right to left, we find *hain dam Yeshua,* meaning, "Behold! The blood of Yeshua."

When presented with the evidence, the journal was baffled and said:

> *Our referees were baffled. Their prior beliefs made them think the book of Genesis could not possibly contain meaningful references to modern-day individuals, yet when the authors carried out additional analyses*

and checks, the effect persisted. The paper is thus offered to Statistical Science readers as a challenging puzzle (Robert Kass, Ph.D., editor of Statistical Science, vol. 9, 1994).

Biblical Review magazine, commenting on the ELS, wrote in an article entitled "Divine Authorship?":

> *The capacity to embed so many, meaningfully related, randomly selected word-pairs in a body of text with a coherent surface meaning is stupendously beyond the intellectual capacity of any human being or group of people, however brilliant, and equally beyond the capacity of any conceivable computing device ("Divine Authorship?" Biblical Review, October 1995, p. 31).*

I believe Paul Crouch's new book uses this discipline of ELS to lead us into an exciting odyssey of discovery concerning prophecies that relate to the end times.

I am sure you will be astounded, as I was, at the things Dr. Crouch has discovered. This book will challenge the most ardent skeptic concerning the miraculous origin of the Bible. It will also thrill and encourage the faith of Christians.

I consider it "must reading" for everyone who is seeking to understand our future.

ONE

Is Time Running Out?

"Are we living in the end times?"

"Is life on earth as we know it drawing to a close?"

"As wars, rumors of wars, technology, population explosions and ecological concerns take their toll on our planet, how much more can this ol' sphere take?"

"Is Jesus really coming soon, or is that just the religious mumbo-jumbo of doom-mongers and fanatics alike? And if He really is coming back, what difference should that make in my life?"

"Should I be afraid?"

Many people have questions about the future, and for good reason. You probably have them, too. It seems that everywhere we look, there are signs that seem to indicate that the end is near.

Many of these signs are discussed in the Holy Scriptures. But even if you aren't familiar with what the Bible says about the end times, common sense may be leading you to similar thoughts.

Just how much longer do we have?

What Jesus Had to Say about the Final Days

The Bible is filled with literally thousands of prophesies, clues and references as to what the final days on earth will be like before, during, and even after the return of Christ Jesus.

In fact, Jesus Himself revealed to His disciples many signs that would accompany the final days. The book of Matthew records a conversation in which Jesus described a number of events which will mark what He called the "beginning of sorrows."

What are the signs that will herald the beginning of the end?

And ye shall hear of wars and rumors of wars: see that ye be not troubled: for all these things must come to pass, but the end is not yet. For nation shall rise against nation, and kingdom against kingdom: and there shall be famines, and pestilences, and earthquakes, in divers places. All these are the beginning of sorrows.

(MATTHEW 24:6–8)

Even though these things mark the beginning of the end, the end is not yet. Are there other signs that will let us know the final days have finally arrived? Definitely. In Matthew 24:14 Jesus says, "And this *gospel of the kingdom shall be preached in all the world* for a witness unto all nations; and then shall the end come."

A few verses later, Jesus reveals yet another hallmark of the end times when he says, "But as the days of Noe were, so shall also the coming of the Son of man be" (Matthew 24:37). What was he talking about? How *were* things in the days of Noah? We read in Genesis 6:5 and 11 that, in the days of Noah, "God saw that the *wickedness of man was great* in the earth, and that every imagination of the thoughts of his heart was only evil continually. . . . The earth also was corrupt before God, and *the earth was filled with violence.*"

So where precisely are we in God's great timeline? The Bible tells us that it is not for any man to know the exact day and time of the return of Jesus Christ, and yet Jesus clearly wanted us to be warned and informed. Jesus explained, "So likewise ye, when ye see these things come to pass, know ye that the Kingdom of God is at hand" (Luke 21:31). "Verily I say unto you, This generation [that sees these signs] shall not pass, till all these things be fulfilled" (Matthew 24:34).

Are we indeed witnessing the beginning of the end? Are wars and rumors of wars on the increase? Today's headlines tell us everything we need to know:

AL-QAIDA STILL THREATENS U.S.

NATO ALLIES, RUSSIA SNARL U.S. WAR EFFORT

POPE CALLS FOR WAR FIRES TO BE EXTINGUISHED

AFGHANISTAN'S ENVIRONMENT RAVAGED BY WAR

What about famines, plagues or quakes? Once again, we have only to turn to current events to get our answer:

"THE OUTBREAK OF DISEASES IN EPIDEMIC IF NOT PANDEMIC PROPORTIONS IS VERY LIKELY."
    —*from a U.N. study of the ramifications of war in the Middle East*

DROUGHT IN ETHIOPIA PRESAGES POSSIBLE FAMINE

FAMINE AND AIDS THREATENING BACKBONE OF AFRICA

WOMEN ACCOUNT FOR HALF OF HIV CASES FOR THE FIRST TIME, U.N. REPORT SAYS

U.S. TO CONTINUE MAJOR FOOD AID TO NORTH KOREA, DESPITE TENSION

16,000 KILLED, 35,000 MISSING AFTER 8.2 EARTHQUAKE ROCKS TURKEY

COFFINS IN STREET AFTER MEXICO QUAKE KILLS 27

And when it comes to an increase in violence, hate crimes and wickedness, we have only to look around our own neighborhoods to see expressions of the depravity of humankind, as these headlines and news quotes confirm:

REBELS CARRIED OUT CAMPAIGN OF CANNIBALISM,
RAPE AND KILLING IN CONGO

DEVIL WORSHIP—A GROWING MENACE

SEXUAL ABUSE AND EXPLOITATION OF CHILDREN ON
RISE THROUGHOUT ASIA

RACE HATE CRIME SOARS IN "MELTING POT" BRITAIN

DOMESTIC VIOLENCE AMONG TEENS GROWING

VIOLENCE AT SCHOOLS SPARKS SHAKE-UP

Clearly, many of the signs described by Jesus are no longer waiting to occur. They are being seen daily in the twenty-first century!

Images from the Future

Jesus' words give us specific things to look for. But we can gather clues from other parts of the Bible as well. Many passages of Scripture paint detailed pictures of what will take place in the final years and days before Christ's return.

To be quite honest, some of these prophectic images have been difficult to fathom until now. Consider what people living in, say, the seventeenth century or in Civil War times must have thought about Revelation's description of a cashless society where commerce is made possible by a numerical identification code embedded permanently on the body (Revelation 13:16–17), or Nahum's vision of lightning-fast chariots jostling each other on "broad ways," their paths lit as if by torches as they speed toward their destinations (Nahum 2:3–4). And think about the likelihood of Jesus' words—the Gospel "preached in all the world for a witness unto all nations"—being fulfilled in a day and age when the world was considered flat, communication could only occur face to face or via courier, and traveling even a hundred miles was a major ordeal!

A hundred years ago these words must have seemed like the stuff of myth and fiction. Today, technology has turned these ideas into current headlines and daily fare.

Cashless society? Commerce by numbers? We're already there thanks to credit and debit cards, PIN numbers, fingerprint scanning technology, even radio-wave-driven speed passes that allow drivers to zip in and out of gas stations and toll booths without reaching for their wallets. Biochips—operational computer chips which can be inserted under the skin with a hypodermic needle— made headlines in 2002 as society debated whether parents should be allowed to imbed their children with the trackable chips as a means of safeguarding them from pedophiles and kidnappers.

Illuminated vehicles jostling at breakneck speeds down a broad way? Even as you read this paragraph, this scene is taking place on thousands of miles of highway in and around countless cities in America and abroad as people jostle, honk and speed their way toward their varied destinations.

Technology has also played a starring role in the fulfillment of Jesus' words regarding the worldwide spread of the Gospel. Computers, modems, television, jet planes, satellites, translation software, printing technology and even the Internet are all helping to bring the Living Good News to virtually every nation and ethnic group.

Let's look at how technology has made possible the fulfillment of yet another prophetic passage of Scripture. I am talking about a prophecy that can be found in the twelfth chapter of Daniel, and its fulfillment is truly an amazing indicator of the end times in which we now live.

In this passage, Daniel is given a vision of the Last Days. In his vision, he receives this instruction: "Daniel, shut up the words, and seal the book, even to the time of the end; many shall run to and fro, and knowledge shall increase."

What do these words mean, and has technology enabled this prophecy to come true?

First let's look at the second part of the verse, the part that tells us that in the last days, people "shall run to and fro, and knowledge shall increase."

Has technology made this possible? You bet it has! Without a doubt, the twentieth century launched an unprecedented information explosion that altered our lives forever, and already the dawn of the twenty-first century promises even greater advances in communication technology. Furthermore, access to knowledge has never been more widespread. Once limited to corporations and educational institutions, then to individuals who could afford their own computers, the Internet is now accessible to virtually every person in the U.S., and even in other countries, via convenient public places such as libraries and Internet cafes. Even our children know how to "run to and fro" on the information super-highway to obtain practially any knowledge they desire!

But perhaps the more intriguing part of the verse can be found at the beginning, where Daniel is instructed to "shut up the words and seal the book, even to the time of the end."

Again, several verses later, Daniel says to an angel, "O my Lord, what shall be the end of these things?" and is told, "Go thy way, Daniel, for the words are closed up and sealed till the time of the end."

Cryptic and intriguing indeed!

Are there parts of the Bible that have, until recently, been "closed up and sealed" to our knowledge?

Could certain words and messages have been concealed in such a way that they would remain undetected until the final days?

Could some sort of code have been used to keep these messages from us? And if so, has God allowed technology to begin to reveal these hidden messages to our generation?

Does the discovery of these hidden messages—what many believe to be the "unsealing of the book" referred to in the final chapter of Daniel—indicate that we are, indeed, living in the last and final days?

I believe that the resounding answer to each of these questions is "Yes!"

Hidden Codes of the Bible

Sir Isaac Newton was one of many great thinkers, past and present, who believe in the existence of secret codes in the Bible, codes that had been hidden for three thousand years. In the past, by using a primitive numerical decoding system, scientists and scholars have managed to uncover simple messages embedded in the text of the Bible. Although these discoveries were interesting, the extent of the coding remained untapped.

Until now.

With the aid of powerful computers, scientists and theologians have been able to uncover *literally thousands of hidden messages* placed strategically throughout Scripture. These messages have been encoded using a relatively simple code called an "equidistant letter sequence."

I promise to explain the code and exactly how it works in the coming chapters. But before I do, let me say that the presence of these encrypted phrases is remarkable for two reasons: First, the very presence of any encoded phrase that makes sense is statistically impossible! Second, these coded phrases are phenomenal because they not only *make sense,* many of them are also *prophetic in nature!*

Indeed, many of these coded messages may reveal the future of the world as we know it. I say this because already scientists have found coded references to the assassination of Prime Minister Rabin, World War II, the Moon landing, the election of Bill Clinton, the Gulf War, the Oklahoma City bombing, the September 11 terrorist attack and even Watergate.

I personally believe the discovery of Bible codes may be the most important discovery of our time because it confirms not only the existence of God, but His in-depth awareness of every detail of our lives.

If the Bible contains hidden details regarding these kinds of twentieth-century world events, what references to events yet to come remain secretly embedded in Scripture and are, even as I write, waiting to be discovered?

What the Codes Mean

Many eminent scholars and mathematicians believe the codes prove, without a shadow of a doubt, that God exists. Many were skeptical, agnostic, even atheistic until the Bible codes proved the existence of an intellect so vastly superior to man that all the theories and arguments of the naysayers collapsed!

Perhaps for those of us who have always known that God exists, the codes say something else: God is aware. He has been, since the beginning of time, intimately aware of everything that has occurred, is occurring, and has yet to occur. The codes prove we are not alone.

I don't know about you, but I find this fact comforting beyond words. Particularly in light of today's troubled times and frightening headlines, I need to know—and my guess is that you do, too—that God is in charge and that He is still in the business of revealing His Plan to those who are willing to trust in Him!

In this day and age, it's easy to find ourselves wondering what the future holds. More importantly, however, is the question "Who holds the future?"

Bible codes give us the answer in amazing ways.

TWO

Bible Codes: The Hidden Signature of God

In the fall of 1994 Michael Drosnin, a reporter formerly with *The Washington Post* and *The Wall Street Journal*, was experimenting with various computer programs, searching the Torah for hidden messages. He had first learned of the existence of these hidden messages—Bible codes—while on assignment in Israel. A self-proclaimed agnostic, Drosnin was skeptical, to say the least!

Then one of Drosnin's searches turned mind-boggling. His program discovered the letters "Y-i-t-z-h-a-k-R-a-b-i-n" spaced in a repeating pattern in a text of Scripture. Finding the name of Yitzhak Rabin, who was then Prime Minister of Israel, encrypted in Scripture was statistically unfathomable! Then Drosnin made a second, more alarming discovery. Crossing Rabin's name in much the same way a crossword puzzle is designed, he uncovered the phrase "assassin that will assassinate."

Drosnin knew full well the significance of what he had found.

After all, scientists had already discovered similar hidden references in the Bible to the assassinations of Anwar Sadat and John and Robert Kennedy.

The difference was this: the hidden messages that revealed the dates and even the names of the assassins of Sadat and the Kennedys had not been discovered until *after* these men had been killed. The existence of the hidden messages was astounding, but their discovery had come too late to change the course of history.

Prime Minister Rabin, on the other hand, was still alive.

Could his life be spared?

Drosnin had to try.

He wrote a letter to Rabin detailing the revelation of the Bible codes. A few days later, in September of 1994, Drosnin met with Dr. Eliyahu Rips, a leading physicist in Jerusalem, and General Isaac Ben-Israel, the chief scientist for the Ministry of Defense.

Drosnin and Rips were not strangers: They had met two years earlier, in the summer of 1992, in Rips's home outside Jerusalem. Rips had shown Drosnin one of his recent discoveries: a similar crossword design of the encoded words and phrases "Hussein," "Scuds," "Russian missile" and "fire on 3rd Shevat." Rips explained that, according to the Hebrew calendar, the 3rd Shevat equated to January 13, 1991, the date Iraq launched the first Scud missile against Israel.

These hidden predictions of the Gulf War had, like many other Bible codes, been discovered "after the fact." But with the discovery of the Rabin assassination prophecy, Rips, Drosnin and others found themselves on a different kind of mission, one of life-or-death significance: to search the Torah for details of the assassination attempt "before the fact" in hopes of saving the life of the Prime Minister. What they found helped a little, but not much. They found a date. It was the Hebrew year 5756, which began in September 1995, twelve months away.

Fourteen months later, on November 4, 1995, Prime Minister Rabin was shot and killed by an assassin.

Drosnin returned to his computer program. A more extensive search of the Bible revealed the following additional phrases: "name of assassin who will assassinate," "Amir," "He struck, he killed the Prime Minister," "Tel Aviv," and "his killer, one of his people, the one who got close."

Incoming reports confirmed that Rabin had been shot in Tel Aviv at close range by an Israeli named Amir.

New Research on an Old Idea

D r. Eliyahu Rips is a leading authority in something called "group theory," the field of mathematics that supports quantum physics. Rips claims to have been an atheist before he learned about the Bible code. Because of his interest in studying the code, he immigrated from Lithuania to Israel to formally research the Bible code and to join the Orthodox Jewish community in Jerusalem as a professor at Hebrew University. In Jerusalem, he began to study the mathematical patterns of the Torah.

In time, Rips was joined by graduate student Doron Witztum and computer scientist Yoav Rosenberg. Rips and his team began to transform the Torah into a computer program. Before long, scientific journals were publishing their findings. Their claim? That the author of the book of Genesis had intentionally encoded, within Scripture, hidden messages that foretold future events. The references to the assassination of world leaders and even to the Gulf War became just a few examples of a growing body of uncovered prophecies.

For example, Rips and his colleagues conducted a particularly fascinating experiment on the first book of the Bible. In what became known as "The Great Rabbis Experiment," Rips and his team mined Genesis to discover, encrypted in crossword fashion, the names of thirty-two renowned sages—both historic and contemporary—along with the dates of their births and deaths. They ran this experiment simultaneously on the Torah, two other original Hebrew texts, and a Hebrew translation of *War and Peace.* The names and dates appeared together only in the Torah. They determined that the odds of this happening were 1 in 10 million.

The results of this experiment were so phenomenal that they captured the attention of Harold Gans, a senior codebreaker who had spent most of his life breaking codes for the National Security Agency in Washington, D.C. Describing himself as "100 percent skeptical," Gans was convinced that Bible codes were a ruse. Writing his own computer program, he set out to duplicate the "Great Rabbis Experiment" conducted by Rips. Gans not only duplicated Rips's findings, but uncovered the names of thirty-two additional individuals as well as the cities in which they were born and died.

The 440-hour experiment made Gans a believer in the Bible code. Indeed, the efforts of this former skeptic and professional code breaker confirmed what Rips and others had been claiming all along: that the Bible contains a crossword puzzle of encrypted words forming a miraculous storyboard of historical events and predictions for the future.

Sir Isaac Newton and "the Riddle of the Godhead"

I ndeed, Rips and his colleagues were not the first to become fascinated with the phenomena of Bible codes.

In the mid-1900s in Prague, Czechoslovakia, Rabbi H. M. D. Weissmandel made the discovery that if he skipped fifty letters, then another fifty letters, and so on, in the Hebrew text of Genesis, the letters spelled out the word "Torah." "Torah" is the Hebrew word meaning "teaching," and most commonly refers to the teaching of God, through Moses, that is found in the first five books of the Bible. After discovering the word "Torah" at a skipped letter sequence of fifty in the book of Genesis, Weissmandel was astounded to discover that the word "Torah" appeared *at the same skipped letter sequence* in the books of Exodus, Leviticus, Numbers, and Deuteronomy—*in other words, in all five books of the Torah!*

Weissmandel, Rips, Witztum and Rosenberg weren't the only scientists researching this phenomena. Mathematicians at Harvard and Yale and scholars at Hebrew University had also been researching the Bible code and confirmed its existence. Even a senior codebreaker at the U.S. Department of Defense had been studying and replicating the Bible code.

The truth is, belief in the Bible code is not a new idea. It has been studied for centuries. Mystics from as far back as the first century have written about their beliefs in the hidden messages of the Torah.

In fact, Sir Isaac Newton considered his pursuit of the Bible code more important than his theory of the universe. His belief in Bible codes not only motivated this English scientist to learn Hebrew, but also led him to spend half his life searching the Bible for what he believed to be the prophecy of human history. The little-known truth is that the majority of Newton's writings focused on his search for hidden messages in the Bible. Newton was, in fact, convinced that the Bible—indeed, that the entire universe—is a cryptogram designed by the Almighty.

John Maynard Keynes wrote in his biography of Isaac Newton that the physicist was obsessed with the Bible codes. According to Keynes, Newton wanted to "read the riddle of the Godhead, the riddle of past and future events divinely fore-ordained."

Newton died before realizing his dream of unlocking the Bible code. He lacked the one thing that might have turned his quest into accomplishment: a computer.

Scientists today don't face that limitation. To borrow a phrase from a hit television show from the seventies, "We have the technology."

With the current state of computer technology where it is, what might be possible? Can we realize Newton's dream of reading "the riddle of the Godhead" as well as the riddle of past and future events?

What untold secrets does the Bible contain, untold secrets to which—thanks to computer technology—we already hold the key?

The Bible Code Theory

For centuries, many Jewish scholars have believed that when God revealed the Torah to Moses on Mount Sinai, He didn't merely pass along important concepts, but dictated each individual letter in a format of continuous characters without spaces or punctuation. For this reason, Jewish scribes for more than three millennia have been painstaking in their efforts to accurately copy the text—down to the letter—in order to preserve its integrity.

A comparison of the various hand-scribed copies of the Torah through the years reveals only nine letters that are not identical in every single copy. The resulting confidence in the accuracy of the Torah lends authority to Bible code research and its findings.

How exactly do researchers look for Bible codes?

Programmers design computer programs to scan the Hebrew text, eliminating all the punctuation marks and spaces so that what remains is an unbroken stream of characters. The computer then pulls out letters at predetermined intervals or "skip sequence"— say every seventh character or every thirty-third or every hundredth. Any number might be used. For example, Yitzhak Rabin's name was discovered at a skip sequence of 4,772 characters. That means there are precisely 4,771 characters between each of the letters of his name.

Once a pattern is discovered that produces a word, the computer uses that pattern to set up a grid or block of text. You have probably seen a very simplified version of this kind of grid in many game books or even on the kids' menu at your favorite restaurant, where the object is to spot hidden words written forward, backward or even diagonally.

In the case of the Rabin prediction, the computer created a block of text 4772 characters long and sixty-four characters high. (If Rabin's name had appeared at a skip sequence of 25, then each row would have been twenty-five characters long. If it had appeared at a skip sequence of one hundred, then each row would have been a hundred characters in length.) Rabin's name was centered in the middle of the matrix, like this:

○ Yitzhak Rabin

Once a matrix such as this one is established, the computer begins to search for related words, phrases, names or dates that appear in close proximity to each other, such as the phrase "assassin that will assassinate" which crossed the name of "Yitzhak Rabin," or—in the case of the Great Rabbis Experiment—the dates of birth and death which were discovered next to the name of each sage.

What are the odds that the phrase "assassin will assassinate" would cross the name "Yitzhak Rabin" in this kind of matrix? According to Drosnin, the odds of this occurring are 3,000 to 1. Mathematicians have determined that 100 to 1 is beyond the realm of random chance.

Timeless Messages from a God Who Knows All

What kinds of messages and predictions have been decoded so far?

Rips found the name "Bill Clinton" crossing "President" just six weeks prior to the 1992 election.

In the book of Genesis, pastor and writer Yacov Rambsel has uncovered codes for "America," "White House" and "G. W. Bush."

In the hidden codes, "Watergate" appears near the name "Nixon." Nearby is the question and answer "Who is he? President, but he was kicked out." How in the world did the writers of the Bible know about one of the key political scandals of the twentieth century?

And how could they have predicted the Great Depression? In another part of the Bible, "Economic collapse" and "depression" appear together with the word "stocks" and "5690" (1929, the year the stock market collapsed).

The words "Man on Moon," "spaceship," and "Apollo 11" were found clustered together in Genesis. Another section of Genesis revealed the Hebrew date for July 20, 1969, the date of Neil Armstrong's historic first step onto the Moon's surface, as well as the phrase "Done by mankind, done by a man" which is eerily familiar considering Armstrong's much-quoted statement, "One small step for man, one giant leap for mankind." Perhaps even more mind-boggling is the fact that these latter codes were hidden beneath the surface text where God tells Abraham, "Look now toward Heaven, and count the stars, if thou be able to number them" (Genesis 15:5).

Rips found details encoded in Genesis that are accurate descriptions of the Gulf War. "Hussein," "Scuds," "Russian missile," and "Hussein picked a day" are encoded in a cluster. And beneath the story of Abraham warring with neighboring tribes in Genesis 14 is the hidden phrase "fire on third Shevat." The third of Shevat equates to January 18, 1991—the day Iraq fired the Scud missile on Israel that prompted the Gulf War.

Doron Witztum, a member of the Rips team, searched for codes referring to the Holocaust and found "Hitler" and "Nazi" encoded together with "slaughter." He found "in Germany," encoded with "Nazis" and "Berlin." "Eichmann" was encoded with "the ovens," "extermination," and "Zyklon B," the name of the gas used in the ovens. Where the surface text reads "an end to all flesh" (Genesis 6:13), he found "in Auschwitz."

In his book *The Bible Code*, Drosnin writes, "No one yet knows if each of us, and all of our past and all of our future, is in some still unknown higher-level code in the Bible, if it is in fact some Book of Life. But apparently every major figure, every major event in world history can be found with the level of encoding we already do know."

War

Missile   Enemy

Saddam

Fire on 3rd Shevat   (January 18, 1991)

Hussein (Picked a Day)

The leaders of World War II are encoded: Roosevelt, Churchill, Stalin and Hitler.

"America," "revolution," and "5536" (1776) were found together. "Napoleon" was found with "France," "Waterloo," and "Elba." "Russia" was encoded with "revolution" and "5678" (1917).

Also found were classic writers. "Homer" was found with "Greek poet" and "Shakespeare" with "presented on stage," "Hamlet," and "Macbeth."

Names of composers, such as "Beethoven" and "Johann Bach" are encoded with "German composers." "Mozart" was found with "composer" and "music." With the name "Rembrandt" was encoded "Dutch" and "painter," and with "Picasso" was found "the artist."

It seems that every major invention has also been recorded in the code. "Wright Brothers" appears with "airplane." "Edison" appears with "electricity" and "light bulb." "Einstein" was found with "science," "they prophesied a brainy person," "he overturned present reality," and "a new and excellent understanding." Also with his name appeared "add a fifth part," which refers to his theory of relativity and the fifth dimension that science now confirms.

"Newton" was found with "gravity" and "Bible code," referring to his diligent pursuit of the discovery of the Bible code.

In 1994, Drosnin found codes of cosmic proportions in the texts of both Genesis and Isaiah. He found "Shoemaker-Levy" (twice encoded), "will pound Jupiter," "8th Av" (July 16, 1994) as well as another coding of the word "Jupiter." Two months later, newspapers reported the greatest explosion ever witnessed in our solar system: a comet—dubbed Shoemaker-Levy after the scientist who had discovered it—had collided with Jupiter "delivering a force of more than a billion megatons, creating fireballs the size of the Earth."

Drosnin writes about the conflict these discoveries created in his secular mindset. Who could have known 3,000 years ago—long before anyone peeked at the sky through a telescope—that these events would take place? Drosnin did not consider himself religious in any sense of the word. He didn't know how to explain what he was discovering. He didn't even believe in God, but these findings were forcing him to challenge his beliefs in the Bible and an intelligence beyond the limits of humanity.

He writes, "The Rabin assassination changed everything. It was the first moment that the Bible code seemed entirely real to me, the moment when what was encoded became life and death fact."

Random Chance or Omniscient Diety?

Try as they might, scientists, mathematicians and theologians—believers and skeptics alike—can offer no logical reason why the codes work.

The Bible code is simply beyond our human intelligence. Our greatest minds cannot even speculate on how the code was created. For man to re-create this kind of code is beyond our current scientific abilities even with the world's most sophisticated computers at our disposal.

"I can't even imagine how it would be done, how anyone could have done it," states Rips. "It is a mind beyond our imagination."

He goes on to describe the Bible as a giant crossword puzzle from beginning to end, with secret codes crisscrossing the entire text vertically, horizontally, and diagonally—a Bible within the Bible!

Another description of Bible codes that I find particularly fascinating actually comes from a Bible code itself. That's right! We have discovered Bible codes providing commentary on the science and existence of Bible codes! In fact, one of the longest and most complex Bible codes that I have seen is a code that talks about the existence of Bible codes! Go to Genesis 20:2, begin with the third letter in the fourteenth word, then count backward five letters at a time and you will find the Hebrew phrase *ha'charek oht shlavi be'rabinyah hynbrb yblv toa irjh.* The translation? "The latticework of equidistant letter sequences for great teaching of the Lord"! Adjacent letters at ten-letter intervals spell "the great perfection of fluent speech"! The odds of this occurring randomly have been calculated to be 100,000,000,000,000,000 to 1.

The fact that the Bible yields such a wealth of hidden messages—while the same experiments conducted on other books produce mostly mumbo-jumbo and relatively few recognizable words—is astounding and miraculous all by itself. When you consider the additional fact that the Bible contains not only *hidden words* but *hidden words that accurately predict the future,* the whole scenario becomes mind-blowing!

Yale professor of mathematics Ilya Piatetski-Shapiro stated, "There is no way within the known laws of mathematics to explain seeing the future. Newtonian physics is too simple to explain a set of predictions this complex and detailed. Quantum physics is also not enough. What we're talking about here is some intelligence that stands outside. . . . I think that is the only answer—that God exists."

One of most astounding clusters of prophetic codes—codes that reveal future events that were unknown at the time the text containing the codes was written—exists within the book of Isaiah. These codes are astonishing because of their quantity as well as

ה ס א ר צ
ה (ה) נ ג ב
ו (ש) ש ב ב
י (ק) ק ד ש
ו (ה) י ז ש
ו (ה) ו י ג
ר (ה) ג ד ר
ו (ה) א מ ר
א (ה) ר ה ם
א (ש) ש ר ה
א (ש) ת ו א
ח (ה) י ה ו
א (ה) י ש ל
ח (א) ב י מ
ל (ה) מ ל ך
ג (ה) ר ו י
ק (ה) א ת ש
ר (ה) ו י ב
א א ל ה י
ס א ל א ב

O Latticework of Equidistant
Letter Sequences for Great
Teaching of the Lord

ס (ה) ו א י ל ד ה ב ן
ו (ת) ק ר א ש מ ו ב ן
ע (מ) י ה ו א א ב י ב
נ (י) ע מ ו ן ע ד ה י
ו (ס) ו י ס ע מ ש מ א
ב (ר) ה ס א ר צ ה ה נ
ג (ב) ו י ש ב ב י ן ק
ד (ש) ו ב י ן ש ו ר ו
י (ג) ר ב ג ר ר ו י א
מ (ה) א ב ר ה ם א ל ש
ר (ה) א ש ת ו א ח ת י

O The Great Perfections of
Fluent Speech

their content. Nearly seven hundred years before the birth of Christ, the prophet Isaiah revealed—in surface text as well as in literally hundreds, perhaps thousands, of Bible codes—vivid details of events that had yet to occur!

The entire book of Isaiah is filled with prophecies, both in surface text and codes. But of all the chapters in this book, the fifty-third chapter in particular is devoted to future events. Actually, astonishingly accurate and vivid prophecies regarding the life and death of the Messiah begin in Isaiah 52:13 and proceed through the end of chapter fifty-three. Within these fifteen verses (a mere 801 letters) Isaiah records in the surface text no less than fifty-seven prophecies about the Messiah, his coming, his ministry and his gruesome death upon the cross. Every one of these prophecies was fulfilled by Jesus Christ!

Even more fascinating is the fact that these same fifteen verses contain literally hundreds of encoded messages regarding Jesus, his ministry, his death and even the names of people with whom he was associated!

Here is a short list of some of the Bible codes discovered within Isaiah 52:13 through the end of the fifty-third chapter:

"Jesus is my name" (53:10, fourth letter, eleventh word, ELS of -20)

"From above, Jesus is my strong name" (53:11, fifth letter, ninth word, ELS of -20) Adjacent letters at the same ELS spell "the lamp (light) of Jevohah"

"Jesus appointed" (52:13, first letter, second word, ELS of 7)

"For mankind" (52:13, third letter, second word, ELS of 7)

"Vision of salvation" (52:14, first letter, fourth word, ELS of 21)

"Pierced in his flesh" (53:5, second letter, sixth word, ELS of 21)

"Water; blood" (53:3, third letter, eighth word, ELS of -18)

Indeed, Jesus' flesh was pierced by studded whips, thorns and nails. A Roman soldier also pierced him in the side with a spear. From that wound flowed blood and water.

In addition, from Isaiah 53:10 emanates a cluster of codes that gives the names of loved ones who were with Jesus when he died. We know from John 19:25–26 that, as he was dying, Jesus was surrounded by his mother Mary, his mother's sister, Mary the wife of Cleophas, Mary Magdalene and the disciple John. In this verse are encoded the names "Mary," "Mary," "Mary," "Salome" and "John."

There are literally hundreds of additional codes in these fifteen verses. Other codes include: Jesus, Nazarene, Messiah, Passover, Galilee, Herod, Caesar, The evil Roman city, Caiaphas, Annas, the disciples, Peter, Matthew, John, Andrew, Thomas, Philip, James, James, Simon, Thaddaeus, Matthias, bread, wine, let him be crucified, his cross, three crosses, the whip, vinegar, blood, water, from the atonement lamb, Mary weeps . . . and many, many more!

Agreeing with the experts, I have concluded that only God could have orchestrated such hidden messages, since it is beyond the capability of mere humans. I have also concluded that God deliberately hid these messages until a time when technology could untangle them as confirmation of God's existence and His presence with us—a new revelation of the Holy Scriptures that God gave to Moses 3,000 years ago on Mount Sinai.

Still Waiting to Be Discovered . . .

B ible code researchers readily admit that they have merely scratched the surface in understanding this phenomena. The more they learn, the more they recognize the unlimited possibilities that lie ahead. Many types of codes must be tested before we realize the vast wealth yet to be uncovered.

The messages discovered so far have been encrypted in what is called Equidistant Letter Sequence or ELS. Equidistant Letter Sequence is just what it sounds like: a code comprised of a sequence of letters spaced an equal distance apart.

The ELS is actually a very simple code, and only one of thousands of possible codes! Indeed, there have been many types of secret codes going back to the beginning of communication. From earliest times, military, political, industrial and personal messages have been written in code to conceal the message from everyone's eyes except the intended viewer. These secret codes have even changed the course of history—consider, for example, Paul Revere's simple code: "One, if by land; and two, if by sea."

When it comes to the Bible, we know that ELS code exists. How extensive is its presence, and are there *other* forms of codes in the Bible that we have yet to discover and unlock?

Acrostics might be considered yet another form of code. Indeed, in his book *Cosmic Codes,* Dr. Chuck Missler examines what he calls a "possible Hebrew acrostic" in the New Testament. He writes: "When Jesus was crucified, Pilate wrote the formal epitaph that was nailed to the cross. The particular wording he used displeased the Jewish leadership, and they asked him to change it. He refused. There are some interesting aspects to this incident that are not apparent in our English translations of John 19:19–22."

Here's what those verses have to say:

> *And Pilate wrote a title, and put it on the cross. And the writing was, Jesus of Nazareth the King of the Jews. . . . it was written in Hebrew, and Greek, and Latin. Then said the chief priests of the Jews to Pilate, Write not, The King of the Jews; but that he said, I am King of the Jews. Pilate answered, What I have written I have written.*

Missler points out that, in Hebrew, if you take the first letter of each of the words in the disputed title that Pilate refused to change, it spells the Hebrew word YHWH, which we pronounce Yahweh! What did Pilate write for display above the head of Christ? An acrostic created from the letters that make up the very name of God himself!

Are there other examples of veiled insights and hidden meanings that we have yet to discover? Many scholars believe the answer to this question is "Yes!"

Of all the possible codes, the ELS codes found in the Bible have garnered the greatest attention. Yet despite hundreds of thousands of hours of research, the truth is that Bible codes are not unlike a giant puzzle with thousands of pieces, of which we can only find a dozen. Many researchers believe that all of history is hidden in the codes—from the details of every life ever lived, to the history of everything that has ever happened. These scholars believe that, within the codes, lies the story of everything that is, was, or will be. They contain more information than the most brilliant scientists and mathematicians in the world can decode.

An eighteenth-century sage by the name of Genius of Vilna once wrote: "The rule is that all that was, is, and will be unto the end of time is included in the Torah, from the first word to the last word. And not merely in a general sense, but as to the details of every species and each one individually, and details of details of everything that happened to him from the day of his birth until his end."

For example, did you know that my name—and my wife Jan's name as well—have been discovered encoded in the Bible? It's true! Go to Genesis 7:13, find the third letter in the eighth word and count forward every fifteenth letter and you will find my name. Adjacent to my name, at the same ELS of 15, is the name of Jan!

You might think that "Paul" and "Jan" are common enough that these names could be referring to anyone, and yet two verses away, in Genesis 7:11, a cluster of codes has been discovered containing nearly a dozen words directly associated with our work. The words that have been uncovered so far—all at the same ELS of 20!—are "TBN," "Paul," "Jan," "Crouch," "Good News," "satellite" "the photo image" (a reference to television?), "film," "praise," "shall be clothed with faith" and finally "information; knowledge."

Is your name waiting to be discovered, alongside details of your life and calling? Many scholars—both religious and secular—believe that it is.

Rips has this to say about the complexity and possibilities inherent in the Bible and its miraculous codes: "It is almost certainly many more levels deep, but we do not yet have a powerful enough mathematical model to reach it." "It is probably less like a crossword puzzle and more like a hologram. We are only looking at two-dimensional arrays, and we probably should be looking in at least three dimensions, but we don't know how."

What Bible Codes Mean to You and Me . . .

I t is both fascinating and chilling to see what Bible codes have to say about events in human history—events that occurred thousands of years after the Bible was written!

With the exception of the Rabin assassination, most of the events I've been talking about—moon landings, political milestones, inventions, accomplishments in music and the arts—had already taken place before we uncovered their "predictions" encoded in the Bible.

After all, until an event occurs, we don't know what names or dates to search for, nor do we have any context of meaning in which to place them. In the mid-1800s, for example, even if we had possessed the technology to find the skip pattern that would produce the letters "zyklonb" encrypted in the Bible, no one could have possibly known or recognized the name of the deadly gas with which the Nazis would attempt to exterminate an entire race nearly one hundred years into the future.

Because of this, Bible codes have provided a mind-boggling commentary on our recent past, but have provided only limited insight into things yet to come.

This is not to say that God has been silent when it comes to future events.

Indeed, in His mercy, God has provided us with extensive commentary on what to expect in the coming days and months. Some of this commentary has, indeed, been uncovered through Bible codes. I will reveal these messages to you in the coming chapters, and my guess is that you will be amazed and comforted by what they say, just as I have been.

Much of what God has revealed to us about the looming future can be found in the book of Revelation. Are you anxious about what tomorrow may bring? Wondering what the advent of the Last Days will mean for you and your loved ones? Then join me on a wondrous adventure as we journey through the book of Revelation. Along the way, we will marvel at God's provisions to help us prepare for everything that is to come, provisions He has given us through His Holy Word—the Holy Word we have been reading for thousands of years, as well as His Holy Word encrypted in strategic hidden messages that are just now coming to light!

THREE

Revelation: A Sneak Peek into the Future

We know that Bible codes exist. We can't use them to tell the future or to precisely predict what will happen in the end times, because we don't always know which words and phrases to plug into the computer. However, we do know that under the surface text of the Bible, God has encoded messages that include details—even dates and names—about the end times. In the next few years, as history unfolds, I have every confidence that we will be able to take names, dates, and phrases straight from tomorrow's headlines, program them into the computer, and find them encoded in the Bible.

We know this because, when we enter end times words and phrases that we already have access to—words like "antichrist," or "mark of the beast" or the number "666," which the Bible refers to—we find them encoded under the surface text. If we only knew other details, dates, and names, I have no doubt that we would also find them encoded, crossing these words or in close proximity to them. What this tells me is that even though God didn't give us the Bible codes so that we could foretell the future, we can use the Bible codes after the fact to confirm His fingerprints on every detail of history in the making.

It makes sense that all things cannot be known to us at this time, because the Bible says that there are things that are not intended for any human being to know until God reveals them to us. Right now, we don't know exactly what to look for, but as God allows these events to occur, I believe we will find more and more details in the hidden codes of the Bible.

In fact, believe it or not, we have discovered encoded messages in the Bible that provide shocking commentary on the horrific events that transpired on September 11, 2001. I promise to give you all the details of this spectacular Bible code before the end of this book. But until then, let me just say that, thousands of years ago, today's headlines were encrypted by an omniscient God under the surface text of His Holy Word. Are tomorrow's headlines there, too, just waiting to be discovered? I have no doubt that they are.

The Bible says that in the end times, knowledge will increase and that more information than ever before will be revealed. This has already been occurring, and we can certainly look forward to even more information being revealed to us in the near future, via Bible codes and other means as well. The Bible is very clear about this.

But what we *do* know, right this moment, is that God is in charge—He knows the future and His plan is authentic. It's not just somebody's opinion. He is in charge and we can rest in that.

Bible codes abound on the topic of the end times. I'm not merely talking about references to assassinations or moon landings, but words and phrases that confirm what we already know about prophecy. I have found these Bible codes to be fascinating windows into eternity, and I want to share some of them with you.

As I mentioned earlier, many books of the Bible refer to prophecy, but the book of Revelation devotes itself entirely to prophecy and, in particular, prophecies concerning the end times. It is, in fact, the unveiling of Christ and of the future, depicting events that "must" come to pass "shortly" or "soon." We have found many codes, and I will point them out to you as we go along, but first—let's take a look at what the Bible comes right out and tells us about our future on earth.

In the coming chapters, I want us to examine the text of the book of Revelation. As we supplement this knowledge with the fascinating study of Bible codes, we will see a consistent picture emerge, one that is vivid and detailed, brimming with images of indescribable horror and images of grace and hope as well.

Revelation "Tells It Like It Is"—and Will Be

W hen it comes to the future, few periods of time have evoked more speculation, curiosity, and controversy than the years that are known as "the end times." The good news is that the Bible is anything but silent on this issue. The Bible contains 66 books, many of which contain references to these last days of life on earth as we know it. One book in particular—Revelation—is devoted in its entirety to prophecy regarding these final days.

In other words, when it comes to satisfying our thirst for knowledge about the future, the Bible is, and has always been, a treasure trove of information.

The book of Revelation is easily the most fascinating book of the Bible. It eclipses the drama of any novel or major motion picture. The plot is complex and action-filled. The cast of characters includes a hero (Christ the triumphant ruler who returns to claim His bride and abolish the forces of evil), a villain (Satan, the archenemy of Christ who, in the pages of this book, makes his final futile attempt to destroy God's creation) and even a villain's evil sidekick (the antichrist is the incarnation of Satan, and Revelation chronicles his initial rise to power as well as his ultimate defeat).

Additional cast include . . .
. . . the seven churches
. . . the four horsemen who deliver the seven seals
. . . the Church—also known as the bride of Christ—which is made up of anyone who believes upon the name of Jesus Christ
. . . the nation of Israel, the chosen people God loves and continues to pursue through the ages
. . . as well as thousands of angels singing God's praises!

Even today, in the new millennium, the book of Revelation has not lost its intrigue. Christians and non-Christians alike continue to be charmed by its mysteries and increasingly are looking to its pages for answers to questions about the future, as evidenced by books appearing on the best-seller lists.

And why shouldn't we be drawn to Revelation? After all, Christ's return to earth and His defeat over Satan is the hope all Christians have anticipated for 2,000 years. The return of the Messiah is the key theme of the Bible and the promise that runs through the entire text.

How the Book Came About . . . and Why

T he Apostle John had been exiled to Patmos, a tiny island in the Mediterranean sea, when Jesus Christ appeared to him in a vision. Jesus not only dictated seven letters to John—letters to seven churches in the part of the world we now know as modern Turkey—but also allowed John to see and hear many astounding things, sounds and images from the Last Days, with the adamant instruction that he was to write everything down.

The year was A.D. 95. Emperor Domitian had banished John to Patmos because of his loyalty to and testimony of Jesus Christ. When God gave these words and images to John, he was the oldest living apostle and as such revered by the early church. He identifies himself as part of the persecuted church who had suffered much at the hands of the cruel emperors of Rome. These emperors had already claimed the lives of Paul, Peter and most of the other apostles.

The way God revealed the book of Revelation to John is certainly a fascinating and unique aspect of the book. Another distinction of

Revelation is this: Revelation is the only book of the Bible that dares to say, "Read me, I'm special!" Revelation is special because it begins and concludes with the promise that anyone who reads it and takes to heart what is written there will be blessed.

Why was the book of Revelation written? So that you and I might be blessed. Intended to be an encouragement when everything around us seems uncertain and frightening, Revelation tells us, in no uncertain terms, to look up and rejoice, for redemption is near!

A Portrait of Victory!

Whatever else Revelation manages to accomplish, it certainly gives us a whole new perspective on Christ, painting a vibrant picture of Jesus as Judge and King. The Gospels paint a different but equally accurate portrait of Jesus; they give us the image of Christ as the Savior of the world, a suffering Jesus who bears the sins of the world. Revelation, on the other hand, shows us Jesus resurrected and victorious, returning to reign over heaven and earth. In the pages of this book, we find vivid images of the final victory as a sword-wielding Jesus takes no prisoners, defeating Satan and brutally crushing his final vile attempt to rule the earth.

Even Jesus' physical description is given. Many of the images are symbolic, which comes as no surprise since Revelation is chock-full of images and symbols. In fact, Revelation contains more than three hundred symbols and images of the final days of Earth as we know it and more than eight hundred references to verses in other New and Old Testament books. Symbolic or otherwise, Revelation offers us powerful images of the risen Christ in His coming glory, images that mirror other images drawn from both the Old and New Testaments.

For example, Revelation tells us that Jesus is "clothed with a garment down to the foot," an important visual since this is the kind of robe worn by the high priests in the temple, representing that Jesus is our high priest.

We are also told that he is "girt about the paps with a golden girdle." This speaks to his strength and authority, since in ancient times only those in authority were girdled in such a fashion.

We are also told that he is human in appearance ("like unto the Son of Man") and that his head and hair are "white like wool, as white as snow," referring to his righteousness.

The imagery intensifies as we are told that "his eyes were as a flame of fire" and "his feet like unto fine brass, as if they burned in a furnace," referring to his indignation and also of judgment and the brazen altar of the tabernacle, where sin was judged.

"His voice as the sound of many waters," describing a deafening roar that all will hear, while "in his right hand seven stars," representing the seven messengers tasked with delivering the letters Christ dictated to John.

We're also told that "out of his mouth went a sharp two-edged sword," which represents the Word of God on the day of judgment, and that "his countenance was as the sun shineth in his strength," which refers to the divine nature of Christ, whose face shone like the sun on the Mount of Transfiguration.

The Final Chapter

Another important symbol we see time and time again in the book of Revelation is the number seven, which, based on the study of biblical numerology, means "to be complete" or the fulfillment of any given thing or event. This is fitting because Revelation does indeed tell the story of the fulfillment or completion of God's plan to redeem mankind. In fact, there are seven major themes running through Revelation, each with seven parts. These are:

1. The seven churches
2. The seven seals
3. The seven trumpets
4. The seven personages
5. The seven bowls
6. The seven dooms
7. The seven new things

I will write more on many of these in the next several chapters, but for now, let me simply make the point that, in every way—even in using seven sets of seven—the message of Revelation is clearly this: It is finished!

Revelation, in essence, finishes the story begun in Genesis. Everything that began in Genesis culminates in Revelation:

In Genesis God creates the heaven and earth; in Revelation Christ creates a new heaven and a new earth.

In Genesis God creates the sun and the moon; in Revelation there is no need for a sun or moon because Christ is the light of the universe.

In Genesis there is the marriage of the first Adam; Revelation tells of the marriage supper of Christ, also known as the "second Adam."

In Genesis sin is introduced to the Garden of Eden; in Revelation Christ abolishes sin once and for all.

What Revelation Means to Us Today

I mentioned earlier that Revelation was created to bless and encourage and even to comfort us—when we read this book, we know how the story ends. We know Who wins the battle for the world and for our very souls!

There is yet another way that Revelation provides us with blessing and encouragement.

As I have said, in the course of the vision he gave to John, Christ dictated seven letters. These letters were messages of love and correction. They were to be delivered to seven churches in Asia.

Archeologists have found remains of these cities and churches. These were real letters, written to real churches. As such, they are fascinating glimpses into not just the first-century church, but also the very heart of God toward real men and women just like you and me. In fact, these seven letters *still* reveal the very heart of God, not just toward people *like* you and me, but toward *you and me* specifically!

I promise you that we will return to the fascinating topic of Bible codes, but before we do, in this next chapter let's take a look at the seven letters to the seven churches. I promise you that as we do we will see God's love toward each of us, no matter where we are in our faith. We will also reap the benefit of his instruction as he admonishes the churches—and us—to make better choices while there is still time before his return.

Christ's letters to the churches—and thus, to you and to me—are yet one more way he is lovingly seeking to prepare us for what is coming next in the glorious End Times Chapter in which we are now living.

Turn the page, and let's see what He has to say to us.

"He that hath an ear, let him hear what the Spirit saith unto the churches" (Revelation 2:29).

FOUR

How Shall We Then Live?

R evelation begins with a bang!

Many New Testament books begin by proclaiming the name of the author: "Paul, an apostle of Jesus Christ by the will of God, and Timotheus our brother," or "James, a servant of God," or even John "the elder." And yet no other book begins with the kind of impact wielded by the opening sentence of the book of Revelation when it claims to be nothing less than this: "The Revelation of Jesus Christ," sent and signified by his angel unto his servant John!

In fact, in two additional verses in the first chapter of Revelation, the true author of this book declares Himself.

In Revelation 1:8, we read these words: "I am Alpha and Omega, the beginning and the ending, saith the Lord, which is, and which was, and which is to come, the Almighty."

And in Revelation 1:11, it is recorded that John heard a voice proclaim, "I am Alpha and Omega, the first and the last: and, What thou seest, write in a book, and send it unto the seven churches which are in Asia." He turns around to see who is speaking to him, and it is Jesus, the Son of God!

Jesus, the Alpha and Omega, has given us the book of Revelation, and for what purpose? I believe that a Bible code discovered in the book of Leviticus sheds light on this matter! In Leviticus 11:38, at the third letter, ninth word, we find the first letter of this stunning phrase, found at an ELS of 91: "Alpha and Omega, the very dimension of grace." Adjacent letters at the same ELS spell "Jesus" and "Jehovah."

Indeed, as we are about to see, grace abounds in these chapters! It is particularly evident in the first three chapters. These are the chapters in which Jesus dictates to John a series of love letters to seven churches in Asia. The recipients of these letters are the congregations at Ephesus, Smyrna, Pergamos, Thyatira, Sardis, Philadelphia and Laodicea—all very real cities in what we now know as Turkey.

These churches are thought to symbolize the church at large— past, present and future. The issues Christ addresses are the same issues present in churches today! In fact, a quick study of church history reveals that these seven issues have challenged communities of believers since the beginning of the church

How do we know that the content of these letters wasn't intended merely for first-century Christians? One of the ways we know is because the most wonderful phrase appears in each of the letters to the seven churches. It is this: "He that has an ear, let him hear." I love this phrase because it says to anyone who reads or hears it, "You got ears? Then listen up! This is for *you*!" This statement also occurs seven times in other books of the Bible. Each and every time, it alerts us to wake up and pay attention; Christ is about to tell us something of great importance.

The Four Goals and Seven Parts of Each Letter

To fully grasp the significance of these seven letters, we need to understand that each letter was intended to meet four different goals or applications:

• Literal—The reprimand in each letter was intended to be applied immediately to the very real problem being faced by the actual church to which the letter was addressed.

• Symbolic—Because the issues raised in each letter are universal issues faced by every church, the seven churches in Revelation can be viewed as symbolic of all churches throughout history.

• Personal—Because these seven messages were also given to any individual "who has an ear to hear," we know they have something of significance to say to you and me!

• Historic—If you examine, in order, the challenges outlined in each of the seven letters, you will find that they address the same problems and phases that have characterized the chronology of the church over the past two thousand years—and in the same order!

So each letter was written with four purposes in mind.

The seven letters are also structured similarly, each made up of virtually the same seven elements (although not every letter contains all seven elements).

The seven "parts" of each letter are as follows:

1. At the beginning of each letter, we find the name of the church. What's more, in each case, the church's name also provides a good description of the character or problem associated with that particular body of believers! Take, for example, the Church at Smyrna. *Smyrna* means myrrh, which is an embalming ointment and represents death. The name is apropos, since the Church at Symrna was under great persecution, even unto death.

2. Also at the beginning of each letter, Christ offers grace and peace. Grace was the traditional Greek greeting. Peace was the Hebrew greeting. Both grace and peace come from God, not human beings.

3. Following his greeting, Christ commends six of the churches for what they are doing well. There is one exception, and it is the church at Laodicea—the "lukewarm" church. To the members of this church He has nothing positive to say.

4. In five of the seven letters, Christ corrects the churches—"But I have something against you." The persecuted church at Smyrna and the missionary-minded church at Philadelphia elicit no reprimand from Christ. But the other five churches are struggling in some manner, and

Christ addresses their problems, which range from lifelessness and compromise to having lost the "first love" passion in their relationship with Jesus Christ.

5. To the five churches to which He has given a reprimand, Christ then delivers an exhortation to turn things around.

6. He makes a promise to those who heed his words and overcome.

7. Finally, Christ again offers grace and peace from He who is, was, and is to come. Grace and peace is clearly a pivotal focus of Christ's message to the churches because he opens and closes each letter with this phrase.

Many Bible scholars believe that these seven letters to the churches may be the most important focus of the book of Revelation, because in the letters Christ gives a distinct description of His expectations for all believers, and He warns us of areas we are prone to neglect. It is interesting to note that each of the churches were taken by surprise both by what they were doing well and by where they were failing. These letters provided a wake-up call to the seven churches of Asia Minor. The letters provide the same wake-up call for Christians today.

He who has an ear to hear, let him hear what the Spirit says to the seven churches! Let's examine the churches one at a time, beginning with Ephesus.

THE SHADOW OF THE APOCALYPSE

Ephesus, the Loveless Church

Ephesus means "my darling, my desired one."

Ephesus was the great metropolis of Asia, where the key religion worshipped the goddess Diana. The church at Ephesus was considered one of the largest and greatest churches of the New Testament era, known for its fervent evangelism that brought in many Jewish converts.

Christ salutes this church with grace and peace. He then commends the church of Ephesus for its good works, patient endurance, and intolerance of evil—particularly their intolerance of evildoers and impostors. These believers also receive praise for resisting the influence of the Nicolaitans, a group of church leaders who believed they had the authority to "lord it over" their congregations. In fact, their name comes from two Greek words: *nikao*, which means to conquer or "lord over," and *laos*, which means the common people.

Yet Ephesus had resisted this trend, and for this they received the praise of their Lord.

What happens next is not unlike being called into your boss's office to hear him say, "Hey, you're doing a really good job, *but* . . ."

It happens when Christ says the key word, "Nevertheless," as He shifts from praise to complaint against this church. His complaint is simply this: "Nevertheless I have somewhat against thee, because thou hast left thy first love." The Judge has one thing against them: despite all their excellent programs and efforts, they had departed from their early heartfelt affection for the Lord!

It appears that the men and women in this church had become so busy with missionary endeavors and good works that they had no time left for a personal relationship with Christ. They had forgotten their love for the Lord. Their weakest link was their devotional life.

To leave a first love is the first step toward a great fall. The Judge entreats them to repent, change their attitude, and return to their first love by doing the things they had done in the beginning.

Christ promises an eternal reward for those who overcome—to eat of the tree of life in the midst of the paradise of God.

What does this portion of the book of Revelation say to you and me? Do we have religion, or do we have a *relationship*? Religion can be good works. Relationship is something else entirely! Jesus wants our relationship with him to be as our "first love." If we have lost that intimacy with Christ—as did the church at Ephesus—all is not lost! Indeed, Jesus offers us grace and peace, lovingly wooing us back into that kind of closeness with Him!

Smyrna, the Persecuted Church

The city of Smyrna was often called the "glory of Asia" because of its idyllic harbor and exceptional temples and architecture. Just forty miles north of Ephesus, the wealthy city of Smyrna was the commercial center of Asia Minor, en route from India and

Persia to Rome. It was also the center for Caesar worship and was home to a large Jewish community that were Jews by nationality only. In reality, they had abandoned their spirituality and opposed Christianity. The community of Smyrna not only persecuted Christians physically, but also boycotted their businesses, leaving them financially destitute.

The essence of Christ's message to Smyrna is this: "You may be persecuted even unto death, but you have eternal life. You may be poverty-stricken, but you are rich in Christ. Do not fear these things which you are about to suffer. The devil will put some of you in prison to test you, but God will turn your testing into approval and reward."

Christ, who has Himself conquered death, promises these believers that if they stay faithful to Him—even unto death—they will receive the crown of life and a martyr's reward. He also assures them that the time of the persecution will be short. He says "ten days," but scholars agree that He's not talking about ten literal days, but using a phrase that symbolized a limited period of time. It is a common belief, in fact, that Christ may have been referring to the number of evil kings under whose rule the church would suffer. Indeed, the church suffered terribly under the reign of ten evil men including Nero (who had Paul beheaded and gave the order for Peter to be crucified upside down), Domitian (who ordered John exiled), Trajan (who had Ignatius burned at the stake) all the way to Diocletian, who was the most evil of the bunch. In this time period, under the persecution orchestrated by these ten men, more than five million believers died for the name of Christ!

Perhaps because He knows what they will have to endure, Christ offers no rebuke to the church at Smyrna. Presenting Himself as One who has already conquered death and will never die again, Jesus acknowledges their suffering, affliction, and poverty for the sake of His name. Christ promises that the overcomer, even if he suffers physical death, will not suffer the "second death," another phrase for eternal death, or spending eternity in the lake of fire and separated from God.

A beautiful image of God's promises to those who endure, even unto death, occurs in Psalms 14:3, first letter, tenth word, at an ELS of -32. It is "God of life." This same Psalm also contains the encoded phrases "Jesus exists," "gift of Almighty," "gift of the Lord," "Messiah for a gift," and "the Creator"! What an awesome reminder of the faithfulness of our Lord!

Pergamos, the Worldly Church

P ergamos means "mixed marriage," a perverted marriage, or a commingling with the world.

Sixty miles north of Smyrna on the Aegean Sea, Pergamos was the capital of Asia and a pagan center of idolatry, demonic religions and Caesar worship. The city boasted lavish temples to Zeus, Athena, Apollo, Bacchus (the god of revelry) and Asclepius (the god of healing). Indeed, the book Revelation refers to Pergamos as a place "where Satan has his throne" and "where Satan lives," perhaps in reference to a massive altar to Zeus that was more than fifty feet high and stood on a colonnaded foundation that was 125 feet long and 115 feet wide.

Christ commends the church for remaining true to the Word of God. Nevertheless, there were those in the church who embraced the doctrine of Balaam and the Nicolaitans, denying the deity of Christ. Many had also been lured into sexual immorality and inter-marrying with idolaters, thereby weakening their Christian resolve.

The message to the Christians at Pergamos is to repent and return to the Word of God or face the double-edged sword of Christ's mouth, symbolizing the Word of God.

As with the churches, Christ makes a promise to those believers in the church who heed His word. His promise here alludes to Christ as the hidden manna, the heavenly bread that God provided every morning to feed the Children of Israel during their wilderness wanderings. There is also a reference to a "white stone," which may represent the diamond embedded in the high priest's breastplate, the "new name" engraved upon it being Christ's.

The temptation to compromise—to embrace wordly values and behaviors—is as much a threat to believers today as ever. The good news is that, even if we are currently engaged in compromise or even sexual immorality, Christ's message is clear: "Return to me—even now—and I will satisfy you!"

Thyatira, the Paganized Church

Thyatira, a wealthy city in Macedonia, was a commercial and pagan center, known for its color dyes and its many trade guilds sponsoring feasts to its idols. Thyatira means "continual sacrifice," and indeed, this name is fitting for a church that still engaged in making sacrifices to idols and thus discounting Christ's work on the cross, which provided the final sacrifice—payment in full—for all of our sins.

Christ commends the church for its charity, service, good works and faith, but again He delivers His criticism, charging the church with tolerating the teachings of the false prophetess Jezebel, Ahab's evil consort who introduced Phoenician cults to Israel in First and Second Kings. As in the days of Jezebel, Thyatira had tolerated false teachings leading to sexual immorality (a symbol of idolatry) as well as the eating of food sacrificed to idols (symbolizing a union of the church with the world). Christ declares that He had given ample opportunity for the church to repent, yet they had not. Then, He declares that He will cast them into great tribulation unless they repent. Christ promises that those who overcome these influences will participate in the leadership of His kingdom and that He will give them the morning star, a reference to His presence in their lives.

Christ counsels those in the church who remain faithful to His Word to "hold fast" until He returns—an explicit reference to His second coming.

Sardis, the Lifeless Church

S ardis means "remnant" and, indeed, in this letter Jesus appears to be calling a remnant of believers out of a spiritually dead environment and into a renewed relationship with him.

Located fifty miles northeast of Smyrna, the city of Sardis was known for its wealth in the textile and jewelry industries. People in Sardis were also known for having a false sense of security and safety. This was due to the location of their city, which was situated at the foot of Mt. Tmolus, a thousand feet above a valley. The city was surrounded on three sides by cliffs that were left unguarded. Sardis didn't seem to learn its lesson when it came to their vulnerability, because in 214 B.C. and again in 549 B.C. the city was invaded by enemy forces who descended the cliffs using footholds carved in the clay surface by rain and wind. What appeared impenetrable was, in fact, more vulnerable than it seemed—a description that can also be applied to the church at Sardis.

Christ's commendation to this church is the shortest of all the churches. In fact, some scholars don't call it a commendation at all, but the beginning of the condemnation. According to Jesus, this church had "a name that thou livest"—a reputation for being alive. That's it. When it came to affirmation, that was the best He could do, the only positive thing He was willing to say!

Christ goes on to say that this church, the congregation at Sardis, was nothing short of spiritually dead. Apparently their focus had evolved from enjoying a personal relationship with Christ to pleasing political leaders. They had substituted formal pageantry and ornate ritualism for true worship, and they trusted in the state rather than in God to meet their needs in times of economic hardship. The church at Sardis was also guilty of nominal Christianity, accepting members into the church without encouraging or requiring any kind of spiritual renewal.

The Lord calls upon this church to (1) wake up, (2) strengthen what remains, (3) remember what it has received and heard (God's Word), (4) keep God's Word and (5) repent. Christ warns that failure to do this will result in judgment instead of blessing at the Lord's return. He cautions them that if they do not repent, He will come as a thief. They will be caught by surprise at His second coming, and their names will be erased from the book of life.

Jesus identifies the true believers in Sardis, the overcomers, as those individuals who have not soiled their clothes with dead works, but are worthy because they trust in the Lord and are clothed in His righteousness. It is interesting that Jesus used clothing as a symbol of dead works or righteousness, an analogy to which the congregation at Sardis would certainly relate since the garment industry was a foundation of the economic health of the city of Sardis.

Christ promises any overcomers that they will be clothed in white raiment, that their names will not be removed from the book of life, and that He will confess them before His Father.

Philadelphia, the Missionary Church

P hiladelphia means "brotherly love."
Located twenty-five miles southeast of Sardis, the city of Philadelphia was an influential center of Greek civilization in the ancient world. The area was plagued with severe earthquakes that nearly destroyed the area.

To the church at Philadelphia Christ presents Himself as:

- "he that is holy," referring to Christ's call to be separate from the world
- "he that is true," meaning genuine, complete, perfect
- "he that hath the key of David," symbolizing Christ's authority
- "he that openeth, and no man shutteth; and shutteth, and no man openeth," representing Christ's ability to open the doors of opportunity for evangelism

The church at Philadelphia was marked by a vitality for life that spurred them to evangelize, thus they were called the missionary church. The Lord says that He has put before them an open door that no one can close. This church fulfilled the Great Commission.

Christ had opened the door of witness at the church of Philadelphia, and it was an open door that no man can shut. The church was not spiritually strong, but it had taken good advantage of its opportunities for witness. It had kept Christ's Word and had not denied His name. Their missionary activities had won many Jews in the city and withstood violent opposition from local Jews who claimed to be the true people of God.

Just as He did with the church at Smyrna, Christ offers no rebuke to the Christians at Philadelphia—only commendation, because they have kept the word of His patience.

Christ promises that He will make heretics worship at their feet and know that He has loved them. He also promises that this church will be spared the horror of the Tribulation period. This promise applies to all Christians who have kept His commandments and endured patiently. He promises to return for His own, and He promises rewards for Christians who overcome. In this letter, believers are clearly identified as God's own possessions and the inhabitants of the New Jerusalem.

To those who overcome, Jesus says; they will be as pillars in the temple of God, and He will write on them His new name!

Laodicea, the Lukewarm Church

T he proud and wealthy inland city of Laodicea was located near Colossae, about forty miles from Ephesus. In addition to being a great commercial and industrial center, Laodicea was a medical center known for its Phrygian powder, which they made into salve to treat eye disease, as well as its production of luxurious black wool.

Interestingly, six miles from Laodicea was a town called Hierapolis, well known for its hot springs. To tap into these springs, Laodicea ran an open aqueduct in an attempt to bring the healing waters from Hierapolis. Many scholars believe the ambitious project fell short of its intended goal because, by the time it reached Laodicea, the water was not only dirty from its six-mile trek, but also unappealingly lukewarm.

To the church at Laodicea, Christ presents Himself as:

- "The Amen," a Hebrew word meaning "final truth." If we want to know more about God, we need look only to Jesus.
- "The faithful and true witness." Jesus is the faithful witness of truth.

- "The beginning of the creation of God." Colossians 1:16 says that "by him were all things created."

This church at Laodicea is distinct from the other six churches in that Christ finds nothing for which to commend it. Actually, the best He can say is that they are "neither cold nor hot"—lukewarm, in fact, much like the waters they piped in from Hierapolis. Jesus states that He would rather they were either hot or cold and threatens to vomit them out of His mouth.

This church thought of itself as rich and in need of nothing. It focused on social propriety and materialism. It may have been involved in a building program or market research or elaborate social events to please its parishioners and make Christianity palatable to the community, but Christ labels it wretched, miserable, poor, blind and naked.

Christ counsels this church:

- "buy of me gold tried in the fire . . ." so that they will be rich. This is an image of salvation, of Christ cleansing the hearts of His own.
- ". . . and white raiment . . ." to cover the shame of their nakedness. White raiment represents being covered with Christ's righteousness.
- ". . . and anoint thine eyes with eyesalve," so that they would no longer be blind. This is, as you can imagine, ironic counsel for believers in a city known far and wide for a salve to treat eye disease.
- Finally, he tells them to "be zealous . . . and repent."

Following this counsel, the letter describes Christ standing outside the door, knocking. This disturbing indictment against the church of Laodicea echoes a wake-up call to Christians today. Christ invites us to hear His voice, to open the door, and to invite Him in. If we do, He promises to come in and commune with us. Today, Jesus still stands, knocking at the door of human hearts, waiting to be invited in.

Finally, Jesus promises all overcomers that they will be granted a seat with Christ on His throne.

Good News for Imperfect Believers

In these seven letters, Jesus offers us a vivid portrait of the expectations, criticism and promises He has for first-century Christians and for you and me as well.

The good news is that Jesus is calling us to repent. Regardless of where we are spiritually at the moment—well-intentioned but falling short, blind and compromising, or even busy and loveless—Christ's message is one of hope and possibility. If we heed His counsel, we will be counted among those who have "overcome," reaping blessings and getting to spend eternity with Him!

What is His counsel to the seven churches and to you and me as well? It is this: Jesus is beseeching you to fall back in love with Him, to fear not, even in the face of persecution, to return to His Word, to stop compromising, to wake up, to be strong, to be rich in Christ, to be clothed in His righteousness, to be zealous, and to open the door when He knocks!

The days are short. He is returning soon. There is no time to waste. I know that one of *my* greatest desires is to be counted among the "overcomers." My guess is that you feel the same.

What do we know so far?

- We know that the end is near.
- We know—from the fascinating study of Bible codes—that God is in charge and that His fingerprints are on every detail of events transpiring in the world today.
- We have also been given—through His letters to seven churches—a detailed portrait of the expectations, counsel and promises that Jesus has for us. We know, without a shadow of a doubt, how He wants us to live our lives in these final days.

So what's next?

Where do we go from here?

In God's great timeline, what remains to be seen? What events of magnitude lie just around the corner?

Let's find out!

FIVE

The Great Escape

Several years ago, I was driving to the store when a woman in the car in front of me had a heart attack behind the wheel. With no one to control her car, the vehicle careened off the road and crashed into a bridge. Other drivers—myself included—were able to avoid being hit by the unmanned car, but it was nevertheless a dangerous moment for many.

Just imagine if, in the space of a single heartbeat, one out of every three cars on the road suddenly became unmanned and careened out of control. What havoc and loss of life would ensue!

Or imagine a jetliner cruising the sky and suddenly spiraling toward certain destruction because the plane was piloted one moment, and unmanned the next.

Perhaps of all the images we have come to associate with the end times, this is one of the most vivid. It is an image of an event commonly known as "the rapture," and it is an image that has been created for us many times through the years via books and movies dealing with the last and final days.

But this image is much more than the wild imaginings of authors and movie producers. Indeed, the Bible itself paints a clear portrait of the rapture—an unprecedented, unannounced moment in time when Jesus Christ will descend to the atmosphere over the earth and, in a twinkling of an eye, all believers in Christ will be caught up to meet Him in the air. The rapture will be the most sensational worldwide event since time on earth began.

One of the reasons the rapture will be so sensational is because not only will living Christians rise to meet their Lord in the sky, but believers who have died will be resurrected to also meet Him in the clouds. Imagine the celebration as graves all over the earth empty and the dead in Christ rise, reuniting with believers who will never taste death, as they join Christ in the air!

Not only will these Christians be resurrected, they will also meet their Lord in new, incorruptible, glorified bodies! Indeed, all Christians—even those who have never died and who are raptured out of cars, planes, offices and even the supermarket—will find their earthly bodies transformed into glorified bodies, just like Jesus' resurrected body, in this glorious moment!

The Apostle Paul described this amazing scene-to-be in this manner:

"For the Lord himself shall descend from heaven with a shout, with the voice of the archangel, and with the trump of God: and the dead in Christ shall rise first: Then we which are alive and remain shall be caught up together with them in the clouds to meet the

Lord in the air: and so shall we ever be with the Lord" (1 Thessalonians 4:16–17).

All of this will happen in what the Bible calls the "twinkling of an
eye." Not a wink or a blink, but a twinkling. A twinkling? What an odd
word. And yet it was not chosen at whim, for while it has been proven
that it takes half a second to wink, and one-tenth of a second to blink,
a twinkle lasts about one-thousandth of a second! That is how fast the
rapture will take place; in the twinkling of an eye it will be over.

Bible Codes Regarding the
Tribulation and Rapture

D oes the Bible contain hidden messages regarding the rapture, the Great Escape that God has ordained for those who
belong to Him? You bet it does!

As I've already mentioned, until tomorrow's headlines become
reality, much of what is hidden in the Bible will remain precisely
that: hidden. But, based on words we already know from Scripture—
words like "rapture" and "tribulation" and "escape"—we have found,
throughout the Bible, a remarkable array of encrypted words,
phrases and sentences that confirm the doctrine of the rapture.
The same prophecies that are written about in the surface text of
Revelation are also described in great detail in equidistant letter
sequences throughout the Bible.

For example, in the sixteenth and nineteenth chapters of Exodus alone, the following phrases have all been discovered clus-

tered together at an equidistant letter sequence of 140: "the twin-kling of the eye"; "the rapture"; "ascend"; "my people, an army of praise"; "joy, strength and wisdom." At the same ELS of 140, these references to Jesus and to God were also discovered: "The Lamb of God"; "Jubilee of the Lamb"; "The Lamb who heals"; and "Jeho-vah, the Prince of Grace," as well as the following references to His kingdom and reign: "land of the Lamb"; "the authentic kingdom" and "the law of the Temple."

Why Will the Church Be Raptured?

W hy rapture? What's the purpose? Why pull believers out of the earth in this spectacular fashion?

The Bible tells us that, in the last days, God will pour out His wrath on an unbelieving and treacherous world. This season of wrath will take place over a seven-year period, intensifying so that the manifestations of God's anger and judgment will be far more devastating toward the end of this season than at the beginning. This seven-year season of wrath is, indeed, called the Tribulation.

In the Gospel of Luke, Jesus gave us signs leading up to the Tribu-lation and the horrible events that will be unleashed. However, He also gave us a Blessed Hope by which we can escape these terrible things that are casting their shadow even as you read this book:

"And when these things begin to come to pass, then look up, and lift up your heads; for your redemption draweth nigh. . . . Watch ye therefore, and pray always that you may be accounted worthy to es-cape all these things that shall come to pass" (Luke 21:28, 36).

In Revelation 3:10, He also makes this promise to the church of Philadephia—and thus to you and to me as well: "Because thou hast kept the word of my patience, I also will keep thee from the hour of temptation, which shall come upon all the world, to try them that dwell upon the earth."

Why would the Lord want to "keep [us] from the hour of temptation" so that we might "escape all these things"? The answer is that this has been His plan for us since time began. In fact, the Bible describes several occasions when God poured out His judgment on ungodly and rebellious people of earth—and time and time again, God has provided means of escape for those who call upon His name.

Consider, for example, when God told Noah to build an ark. As a result of God's wrath unleashed upon an ungodly world, the earth was covered by a great flood. However, by instructing Noah to build a huge structure that would ride the waves, God not only provided a way of escape for Noah and his family (and anyone else who would heed Noah's warnings), God even used the judgment waters themselves to lift Noah to safety! Some Bible scholars see a type of rapture in the "lifting up" of Noah and his family to safety.

When the perverted twin cities of Sodom and Gomorrah evoked God's wrath, God unleashed burning sulfur and fire that leveled the cities—but not before pulling Lot and his family out of danger.

When the time came for God to pour out His wrath on Egypt because of their idol worshipping and horrible blasphemies against God and His people, God delivered the entire nation of Israel to safety before destroying the Pharaoh and his armies.

God has always removed His faithful before the onslaught of His wrath. And in like fashion, the time is coming soon when Christ will rapture His own before He pours out final judgment on Earth.

How do we know this? For one thing, if believers were destined to go through the Tribulation, our Lord would not have said the things He did: warning us to pray so that we might be counted worthy to escape, encouraging us to look up because our redemption is coming, promising to keep us from the hour of trial.

There are many other passages in the Bible that tell us the same thing. The Great Escape of believers from the time of trouble is based on biblical doctrine and not just on wishful thinking.

In his letter to the church in the city of Thessalonica, Paul refers to Jesus as the one "which delivered us from the wrath to come" (1 Thessalonians 1:10) and goes on to write: "The day of the Lord so cometh as a thief in the night. . . . But ye, brethren, are not in darkness, that that day should overtake you as a thief. Ye are all the children of light, and the children of the day. . . . Therefore let us not sleep, as do others, but let us watch and be sober . . . putting on the breastplate of faith and love; and for an helmet, the hope of salvation. For God hath not appointed us to wrath, but to obtain salvation by our Lord Jesus Christ" (1 Thessalonians 5:2–9).

Grant Jeffrey, in his book *Final Warning*, refers to this same Great Escape when he quotes the writings of Ephraem the Syrian from the year A.D. 373: "For all the saints and Elect of God are gathered, prior to the tribulation that is to come, and are taken to the Lord lest they see the confusion that is to overwhelm the world because of our sins."

An interesting Bible code that speaks about "escape" is found in Genesis 7:5, in the midst of the verse describing Noah's family entering the ark so that they might be saved from the floods of the wrath of God. In this verse, begin with the third letter in the fifth word, then count forward every ninth letter. Here is spelled the phrase "many sons escape." If you begin at the first letter and count every fourth letter it spells "In God." Even more amazing is the fact that adjacent letters at the same ELS spell "with hope and expectation, the gift of the Lamb."

God is in the business of delivering those who call upon His name. And when it comes to the great story of the last and final days, can there be better news than this? Believers may suffer at-tack by many adversaries in this world, but we will never be on the receiving end of God's wrath!

כלאשרצוה ו
יהוהוונחב ן
ששמאותשנ ה
והמבוילהי ה
מיסעלהאר ץ
ויבאנחוב נ
יוואשתוו נ
שיבניואת ו
אלהתבהמפ נ
ימיהמבול מ
ןהבהממההט ה

O Many Sons Escape

When Will the Church Be Raptured?

There are many excellent scholars who hold various beliefs on the precise timing of the rapture of the Church.

For example, there are those who believe in a *mid-Tribulation* rapture, believing that Christ will rapture the Church midway through the Tribulation period (three and one half years into the seven years).

Post-Tribulation scholars believe that Christ will not rapture the Church until the end of the seven years.

I personally hold to a *pre-Tribulation* theory, believing that Christ will rapture the Church *before* the seven-year Tribulation begins.

Why do I believe in a pre-Tribulation rapture? There are three reasons:

- **God did not appoint us to wrath!** We've already discussed this, but it is worth mentioning again. The whole purpose of the rapture appears to be to provide a means of escape so that the church does not experience the wrath of God poured out upon an ungodly world.

  Remember Jesus' promise to the Church—the historical church at Philadephia as well as the Church today—in Revelation 3:10–11? "Because thou hast kept the word of my patience, I also will keep thee from the hour of temptation, which shall come upon all the world, to try them that dwell upon the earth. Behold, I come quickly."

And His admonition, recorded in Luke, for you and me to watch and pray so that we might be "counted worthy to escape all these things that will come to pass."

Intended as a means of escape for the believing Church, the rapture must occur before the events take place from which the Church is being spared!

· **Scripture points to a pre-Tribulation rapture: There are sixteen references to the Church within the first three chapters of Revelation, but not one mention of the Church in chapters four through eighteen, which cover the Tribulation period.** Since the Church is so prominently featured in the first three chapters of the book of Revelation—and not mentioned at all in chapters four through eighteen—it makes sense to assume that the Church, at this point, has already been caught up to heaven.

· **Scriptures paint a beautiful portrait of the raptured Church in heaven, at the throne of God, singing and praising as the first "seal" is broken, the act that signifies the inauguration of the Tribulation.**

We find this image in the fifth chapter of Revelation where we read,

> *And they sung a new song, saying,*
> *Thou art worthy to take the book,*
> *and to open the seals thereof:*
> *for thou wast slain,*

and hast redeemed us to God by thy blood

out of every kindred, and tongue, and people, and nation;

and hast made us unto our God kings and priests:

and we shall reign on the earth.

The seals they are referring to are the seven seals that Jesus breaks, each unleashing a new facet of God's judgment upon the earth. We will talk about the seven seals later, but for now let me just say that they are not the stuff of pleasant dreams! Death, discord, famine, earthquakes, darkness and bloodshed are among the judgments visited on those remaining on earth as Jesus breaks the seven seals, one at a time.

But for now, simply notice that the redeemed of the Lamb of God from all generations and walks of life are already in Heaven before the first seal is opened. Only after this first seal is opened can the Tribulation begin. Since literally thousands of thousands of believers are already in Heaven, it makes sense that the rapture takes place before the opening of the seals.

So far, we've answered the following questions:

What is the rapture? An unprecedented and instantaneous reunion of God's people with their Lord as believers—living and dead—are called out of the earth to meet up with Jesus in the sky!

Why will the church be raptured? To escape the wrath of God.

When will the church be raptured? Before the first seal is broken, signaling the beginning of the Tribulation.

There is a third question that begs to be answered, and it is this: Are the rapture and the Tribulation still a long way off, or could they happen at any moment?

How Soon Might This Occur?

F rom the time Jesus walked the earth to this day, believers have asked the question: When will the rapture of the Church take place? I have been asked this question thousands of times over the years. My answer is always the same.

The Bible clearly states that the Gospel must first be preached in all the world; only then can the end come.

Indeed, nothing could be plainer than this statement by the Lord Himself: "And this gospel of the kingdom shall be preached in all the world for a witness unto all nations; and then shall the end come" (Matthew 24:14).

Has this gospel of the Kingdom been preached to all nations around the world?

Certainly, when it comes to reaching individuals with the Good News of Jesus Christ, our generation still has a lot of work to do. However, no one can deny that, since the time of the Apostles, the gospel has been taken around the world, impacting every nation on Earth! Indeed, the efforts of many ministries, including Trinity Broadcasting Network (TBN), have helped to accomplish this task in what I believe is fulfillment of the prophecy that Jesus gave in the book of Matthew. This—along with Israel becoming a nation again in 1948 after centuries of exile—remains one of the most important signs of the end times.

In other words, I believe the rapture could happen at any moment.

What Will Life Be Like after the Rapture?

For believers, the time following the rapture will be one of joyous celebration. All you have to do is read the fourth and fifth chapters of Revelation to catch a glimpse of the excitement, energy and celebration as saints and angels gather 'round the Throne of God and "sing a new song" of worship, adoration and praise!

We also know that, after the rapture, believers will be doing all of this celebrating and worshipping in new bodies that will never deteriorate nor grow old—glorified bodies not unlike the resurrected body of our Lord Jesus.

How do I know this? Because not only does the Apostle John write in 1 John 3:2 that "when he shall appear [to rapture the Church into Heaven], we shall be like him," but Paul also wrote about our new bodies in one of his letters to the church at Corinth: "Behold, I show you a mystery; We shall not all sleep [die], but we shall all be changed, in a moment, in the twinkling of an eye, at the last trump: for the trumpet shall sound, and the dead shall be raised incorruptible, and we shall be changed. For this corruptible must put on incorruption, and this mortal must put on immortality. So when this corruptible shall have put on incorruption, and this mortal shall have put on immortality, then shall be brought to pass the saying that is written, Death is swallowed up in victory. O death, where is thy sting? O grave, where is thy victory?" (1 Corinthians 15:51–55).

Wow! That scripture strikes to the core of my being. If you and I believe on Christ Jesus, we will be resurrected, made immortal, never again to taste death!

What else do we know about life after the rapture?

We know that two thousand years ago, at His last supper with the disciples, Jesus comforted his followers with these very words: "Let not your heart be troubled: ye believe in God, believe also in me. In my Father's house are many mansions: if it were not so, I would have told you. I go to prepare a place for you. And if I go and prepare a place for you, I will come again, and receive you unto myself; that where I am, there ye may be also" (John 14:1–3).

So we know that, following the rapture, you and I will be celebrating. We will have new bodies. And we will be forever with Jesus, in a place he has lovingly prepared for you and me! This is what life will be like—at least for those who have accepted Jesus Christ as their Savior.

For those who haven't, life will be altogether different. After the rapture, the nations of the world, small and large, will declare national emergencies as governments grapple to explain why millions of people have suddenly disappeared. Martial law will be put into effect immediately, severely disrupting business as usual on planet Earth. Life as we've known it will change forever as families grieve the disappearance of loved ones and ponder their own futures in a world suddenly gone awry. Suffering will increase as plagues, earthquakes, death, discord and destruction are unleashed in the world. Physical persecution, social stigma and financial ruin will be heaped upon anyone who comes to realize the significance of being "left behind" at the rapture and as a result accepts Jesus at this eleventh hour.

Indeed, there will be those who, during the Tribulation, cry out to God despite certain persecution. Their newfound faith will be severely tested. The good news is that, to those who prevail, Christ offers life.

Indeed, at the end of the seven-year Tribulation, Jesus returns in majesty. In Revelation 19, we see Jesus returning to earth to do battle against the forces of evil. He embraces those who have accepted Him as their Savior during the trials of the Tribulation, and sets up His Kingdom to rule here on earth for a thousand years. Some scholars believe that even those who have given their lives as martyrs will be resurrected to reign with Jesus Christ and the saints for a thousand years.

What about the Nation of Israel?

If you are familiar at all with the Old Testament, it is clear that the nation of Israel is the first love of our Holy God. Will the nation of Israel be included in the rapture?

Yes and no.

Individually, any person—Jew or Gentile—who accepts Jesus Christ as Lord is considered a part of the Church, and will be caught up into the sky to meet Jesus in the Great Escape.

Any Jew who has not accepted Jesus Christ as Lord is not part of the Church, and will not be raptured. However, he or she still is part of the nation of Israel which remains, as we are about to see, very much front and center in God's great plan for the last and final days.

In fact, a passage in the book of Jeremiah paints a stirring picture of the destiny of the nation of Israel. In this passage, we see a stubborn Israel being chastised for her rebellion by being left behind to experience the Great Tribulation. We also see this same nation, ultimately, rescued and embraced by the God who has loved her for centuries.

The passage begins when the prophet warns the people of Israel to repent and return to God, but they refuse. In fact, Israel does more than merely refuse: she openly rebels, provoking God to anger! As a result, God promises to deliver her into the hand of the King of Babylon for seventy years, in which time she will experience persecution, famine and pestilence.

What I find most stirring about this passage is the motive behind the actions of God: He loves Israel. Even though he allows Israel to suffer at the hand of the King of Babylon, God makes this tender promise:

> *Behold, I will gather them out of all countries, whither I have driven them in mine anger, and in my fury, and in great wrath; and I will bring them again unto this place, and I will cause them to dwell safely: And they shall be my people, and I will be their God: And I will give them one heart, and one way, that they may fear me forever, for the good of them, and of their children after them: And I will make an everlasting covenant with them, that I . . . will put My fear in their hearts, that they shall not depart from me. Yea, I will rejoice over them to do them good, and I will plant them in this land assuredly, with my whole heart and with my whole soul. For thus saith the Lord; Like as I have brought all this great evil upon this people, so will I bring upon them all the good that I have promised them.*
>
> (JEREMIAH 32:37–42)

What a beautiful picture of God's stubborn love for Israel!

Bible Codes Found in Isaiah and Daniel
Regarding the Tribulation and Rapture

T he book of Exodus is not the only book in which Bible codes
describing the Tribulation and rapture have been discovered.

A number of coded messages have been uncovered in the 26th
chapter of the book of Isaiah, encrypted in the portion of text
where Isaiah has this to say about the Last Days:

> *We have not wrought any deliverance in the earth. . . . For behold, the*
> *Lord cometh out of his place to punish the inhabitants of the earth for*
> *their iniquity: the earth also shall disclose her blood, and shall no more*
> *cover her slain.*
>
> (ISAIAH 26:18–21)

The codes found encrypted here include "sons of light delivered,"
"in their rapture," and "all upright."

There is another book in the Bible that discusses the Last Days
in both surface text and also in ELS. It is the book of Daniel, particularly the seventh and twelfth chapters.

In chapter twelve, for example, Daniel described the Tribulation
in these words: "And there shall be a time of trouble, such as never
was since there was a nation, even to that same time" (Daniel 12:1).

Regarding the rapture, he writes these words, spoken to him in
a vision by a heavenly messenger:

> *And at that time thy people shall be delivered, every one that shall be*
> *found written in the book. And many of those that sleep in the dust of*

בדנזכירשמן○מתיםסבליחיורפאיסבליקמולכןפקדתותשמידמותאבד
והרהתקריבל○דתתחילתוזעקבחבליהכןזהייונומפניךדיההוההרינוחל
פרכיטלאורת○לדוארקרפאיםתפילללדעמיבאבחדריךוסגרדלתיךבע
אתכסהעודעל○רוגיהביומההואיפקדיהוהכחרבוהקשהוהגדולהוה
והנצרהלרגע○סמאשקנהפןיפקדעליהליהלויוסאצרנהחמהאיןלימי
יעקביציקופ○חישראלומלאופניתבלתנובהה☐מכתממכהוהכהואסכה
רחטאתובשו○כלאבנימזבחמכאבניגרמנפצותחל☐איקמואשריוחמני
באותמאירות○ותהכילאעמבינותהואעלכןלא☐רחמנועשהוויצרול
ומהההואיתקע○שופרגדולובאוהאבדיסבארק☐אשורוהנדחיסבארצמצ
אשמניסהלום○יןהנהחזקואמקלאדניכזרמב☐דשערקטבכזרסמיסכ
עלראשאגיאשמ○יסכבכורהבטרסקיקאשריראההרהאהאותהבעודהצכפו
ולגברורהמשי○ימלחמהשערהוגמאלהביין שגווסשכרתעוכהן○בניא
ורהדעהואתאתמיביןשמעיעהגמולימחלבעתיקימשדיסכיצולצו○ולצ
הניחולעיףונזאתהתהמרגעהולאאבואשמוועוהיהלהמדבריהוהצו○צוצ
אנשילצוןמשליהעמהזהאשרבירושלמכיאמרתמסכרתנוברית○אתו

○ Sons of Light Delivered
◇ In Their Rapture
☐ All Upright

the earth shall awake, some to everlasting life, and some to shame and
everlasting contempt. And they that be wise shall shine as the bright-
ness of the firmament; and they that turn many to righteousness as the
stars forever and ever.

(DANIEL 12:1–3)

What is beyond amazing is the fact that, spaced twenty letters apart throughout this chapter, are words that mirror Daniel's message—words like "ascend" and "light" and "splendor" and even phrases such as "shall rise" and "shall be priests."

Phrases of even greater detail have been discovered throughout the same chapter at other equidistant letter sequences. For example, "Lift up My precious people to heaven" has been discovered, as has the phrase "To the house of life." Other amazing phrases encoded in the twelfth chapter of Daniel include "The Prince of life";

"My everlasting God"; "The perfect sin offering"; "The great songs of the hereafter"; "shall be the songs of power"; and "The blood, it shall be wonderful healing for all" as well as "Behold! Instant healing." "I am the perfect Father"; "This is the Lord speaking from the first position," as well as the intriguing phrase "the glittering encampment of the golden angels."

Chapter 7 provides another stunning collection of encoded words related to the final days. In this chapter, we find the following phrases: "You shall escape"; "Raptures"; "The pure ascend"; "Shall be concealed by grace"; "Shall be delivered"; "Shall be concealed . . . from the Tribulation"; and the truly sobering and amazing phrase "the evildoer shall be left behind."

You may recall from Chapter 1 that Daniel is the one who recorded these words of instruction: "But thou, O Daniel, shut up the words, and seal the book, even to the time of the end; many

בעארבעהמלכין יקום
ונזמןארעאו|י|קבלונם
לכותאקדישיעליוני
זויחסנונמ|ל|כותאעד
עלמאועד(ע)למעלמיאא
דינצבי(ת)(צ)באעלחי
ותארבי(י)תאדיהותש
ניהמןכל(ה)ו|ז|דחילהי
תירהשני(ה)דיפרזלוט
פריהדינ(ח)שאכלההמדק
הושאראב(ר)(ג)ליהרפסה

○ The Pure Ascend
□ Raptures

shall run to and fro, and knowledge shall be increased. . . . Go thy way, Daniel: for the words are closed up and sealed till the end of time. Many shall be purified, and made white, and tried, but the wicked shall do wickedly: and none of the wicked shall understand; but the wise shall understand" (Daniel 12:4,9–10).

What words were shut and sealed until the time of the end? And are Bible codes God's way of allowing these words to be unsealed for you and for me? Will we be counted among the wise, taking these words and allowing them to increase our understanding? Or will we ignore what they are trying to tell us, choosing ignorance and eternal death instead?

What This Means to You Today

This is the hope that the book of Revelation offers: The hope of a Great Escape from the wrath of God, as well as the promise of an eternity of celebration in the place that Jesus has lovingly prepared for you and for me.

In the following chapters, we're going to continue our look into the future via the book of Revelation. But before we do, let me ask you one question: If the rapture took place this very hour, do you know what your fate would be? Would you join other believers and find yourself transported in the twinkling of an eye into the presence of the God you know and love? Or would you find yourself left behind, facing an onslaught of the greatest terrors known to mankind since the beginning of time?

You don't have to wonder. You can be sure. It's not rocket science, nor does it require a superhuman effort on your part. All it requires is simply opening your heart and accepting the gift of salvation that Jesus has provided for you.

You know, earlier in this chapter I wrote about a few of the ways that God has lovingly rescued from wrath and judgment those who call upon His name: He told Noah how to build an ark. He sent an angel to draw Lot and his family to safety. He brought the nation of Israel out of Egypt. And one day soon He will rapture believers to safety and out of the horror of the coming Tribulation.

But by far the most amazing and profound "rescue" that God ever orchestrated was when He made provisions to save you and me from the crushing impact of His Holy wrath and judgment by heaping it, instead, onto the broad shoulders of His beloved Son. As Jesus suffered on the cross—a monstrous form of execution—He took upon himself the wrath of God so that you and I would be spared.

The provision is there. All we have to do is receive it!

If you have not embraced all that God has provided for you through Jesus Christ, you can do it today, right now. Do you want to know, beyond a shadow of a doubt, where you will be when the rapture takes place? Where you will spend eternity? Then pray this prayer with me right now: "Jesus, thank you for taking, upon yourself, the penalty and judgment for the sins of the world and my sins as well! I accept all that you have provided for me through your death on the cross and receive you into my life and my heart as my Lord and Savior."

If you have prayed this prayer today, don't keep it a secret! Let someone know, such as a pastor, friend or family member with a faith in God. Or let one of our prayer partners here at TBN know about your decision. We would love to rejoice with you and pray with you over the phone.

Here are other encoded messages that I find so amazing. I'm sure you will too.

Rapture Messages Encoded in the Sixteenth and
Nineteenth Chapters of Exodus

The following messages—all encoded at 140 ELS—were found clustered together in the sixteenth and nineteenth chapters of Exodus:

> The twinkling of the eye
> The rapture
> Ascend
> My people, an army of Praise
> The people shall live
> The life of power
> Joy, strength and wisdom
> Jubilee of the Lamb
> The Lamb who heals
> The Lamb of God
> The Shekinah God
> Jehovah, the Prince of Grace
> Land of the Lamb
> The authentic Kingdom
> The law of the Temple
> The lifted up God
> The great God
> The Lamb of Jubilee

Rapture Messages Encoded in the Twelfth Chapter of Daniel

The following messages refer to the rapture, and were discovered at -20 ELS:

Shall rise

Ascend

Shall live

Shall be priests

Life

Light

Splendor

My Messiah

Army of praise

Rapture Messages Encoded in the Seventh Chapter of Daniel

You shall escape

You shall escape

Rapture

The pure (noble) to ascend

Shall be concealed by grace

Shall be delivered.

Jesus; Yeshua

Shall be concealed (rescued)

Following this insight at the same ELS is another phrase that tells us from what we will be concealed: From the Tribulation

The evildoer shall be left behind

Rapture Messages Encoded in the Twenty-sixth Chapter of Isaiah

Rapture (The phrase "Spirit of Jesus," which is underlined, intersects this insight)

Ascend

Escape

Escape (rescue)

Escape

Sons in the Light of the Lord, escape

Time of evil

Evil Tribulation

More Rapture Messages Encoded in the Twelfth Chapter of Daniel

Lift up My precious people to Heaven

To the house of life

The Prince of life

My Everlasting God

The perfect sin offering

The redeemed (chapter) of graciousness

Savior

Shall be the songs of power

Praise God!

The great songs of the Hereafter

Behold! Instant healing

The blood, it shall be wonderful healing for all

Day for the Groom

(Continued)

The glittering encampment of the golden angels

I am the perfect Father

This is the Lord speaking from the first position.

Isaac, the Prince

The city of Shiloh

SIX

At the Throne of God

I would love to see what a crack team of Hollywood's best special effects artists could do with the forth and fifth chapters of Revelation! What a scene is presented here as John finds himself caught up into Heaven and standing before the very throne of God.

This scene has it all: thunder and lightning, voices and fire, music and incense, winged, chanting living creatures, robed elders and a throned Being so brilliant that His physical description cannot be grasped: the best John can do to describe this Being is to compare Him to precious stones and jewels encircled by an emerald rainbow! This is the very throne of God.

Best yet, what takes place here is not the stuff of fiction: What John witnessed in his vision will take place in reality at some point in the rapidly approaching future!

Let's take a closer look at the participants in this unfolding drama. Around the throne of God there are twenty-four elders—

each wearing a white robe and a golden crown and sitting on a throne of his own. Opinions vary among Bible scholars and eschatologists as to who these elders are. I and others believe that they may represent the leaders of the twelve tribes of Israel and the twelve apostles. What we know for sure is that these are twenty-four leaders in Heaven with God.

Also present are four seraphim in the form of the four Living Creatures. These are amazing beings indeed, one like a lion, another like a calf, another with the face of a man, and a fourth like an eagle. Each seraphim has six wings and is full of eyes all around and even within. Two men—John and Isaiah—visited the throne of God in visions and each described these same winged seraphim, standing at the throne of God and crying "Holy, holy, holy!"

The other element present at the throne is twelve lamps burning with fire. Throughout the Bible, fire is often used to represent God's Holy Spirit, and this reference is no exception. Indeed, in Revelation 4:5 we read that "there were seven lamps of fire burning before the throne, which are the seven Spirits of God."

Seven spirits of God. What an interesting phrase! Isaiah 11:2 sheds some light on this phrase as Isaiah writes about seven different facets of the Holy Spirit: "The Spirit of the Lord shall rest upon Him, the Spirit of wisdom and understanding, the Spirit of counsel and might, the Spirit of knowledge and of the fear of the Lord." It appears, then, that these are the seven Spirits of God: The Spirit of the Lord, the Spirit of Wisdom, the Spirit of Understanding, the Spirit of Counsel, the Spirit of Might and the Spirit of the Fear of the Lord.

So at the throne of God we have God himself, twenty-four elders, four seraphim and the Holy Spirit in his multifaceted splendor. There is also a cast of thousands upon thousands made up of angels and saints (I believe many of them recently raptured) and every creature in heaven and earth and under the sea.

Then John notices that in the right hand of the Being on the throne is a scroll. The scroll is covered front and back with writing, and sealed with seven seals.

What is written on the scroll? Theories include the Old and New Testaments, the title deed to earth, God's sentence against those who have opposed Him throughout history. Whatever is the exact nature of the contents of the scroll, it's likely that the scroll contains God's will and testament regarding the future of Israel and of the earth—not history *in* the making, but history *before* the making, and in the hands of the Maker of the Universe. Indeed, in Roman times, wills were customarily sealed with seven seals, each signifying the mark of a separate witness. The important thing is that, as always, God is in control. The future is in His hands.

Suddenly a strong angel steps forward and proclaims, in a loud voice: "Who is worthy to open the scroll and to loose its seals?"

Silence follows. Not a single man, woman, angel, elder or creature can claim to be worthy to open the seals of the scroll. John begins to weep, perhaps with disappointment, perhaps because the future of the world hangs in the balance, waiting for the seals to be broken and the scroll read. How can God's will be executed if it can't even be read? It's as though Heaven and earth hold their breath and wait.

The Lamb Is Worthy

S uddenly one of the elders speaks to John and says, "Weep not: Behold, the Lion of the Tribe of Judah, the Root of David, has prevailed to open the scroll and to loose its seven seals." This pronouncement is echoed in a Bible code found in Daniel 12:1 (second letter, seventeenth word, ELS of -23) which reads: "the strong lion of David." And now, in heaven, at the proclamation of the elder, Jesus Christ steps forward.

But what an image of Christ!

He does not appear as a lion, as the elder announced. Instead, Christ appears as a Lamb, scarred with the wounds of death and then resurrected to life. We know that the Lamb is living—after all, He is standing in the midst of the throne—but He bears the marks of having been sacrificed at an earlier date. John writes, "And lo, in the midst of the throne and of the four living creatures, and in the midst of the elders, stood a Lamb as though it had been slain."

The slain Lamb! What a familiar image! After all, God has always required a blood sacrifice to atone for the sins of man. For generations upon generations, the blood sacrifice that He required was that of a lamb. Indeed, each year the Jews selected a perfect lamb—flawless in every way—and slaughtered it upon an altar to "pay for" their sins. After Christ's death on the cross, God no longer required the sacrifice of a lamb. Indeed, a much greater sacrifice had been provided, this time by God Himself, toward the redemption of the people He loved. On the cross, Christ became the sacrifice for every sin ever committed and every sin yet to be committed. He became, for each of us and until the end of time, the Sacrificial Lamb.

But this Lamb is not to be pitied! Indeed, in addition to the scars of being slain, John says that the Lamb has seven horns—representing power—and seven eyes—representing omniscience and the fullness of the Holy Spirit.

What a beautiful portrait of the heart and ministry of Christ! Even though He is the King, even though he has all power, even though He sees everything that has and will occur, and even though He is empowered by the fullness of the Holy Spirit, Christ still went as a Lamb to the slaughter. Why? Because He wanted to do His Father's will, and because He desired to provide the means so that, as you and I believe on His name, we will not perish but have everlasting life!

This is the One—the only One—worthy of breaking the seals and bringing to fruition the final chapters of God's will—the final settlement of the affairs of earth and of the redemption of mankind!

A Look at the Big Picture

Christ does, indeed, open all seven seals on the scroll. And as he does, a volley of cataclysmic and catastrophic events are unleashed on earth, the likes of which have never been seen. Each time a seal is broken, chaos and disaster are the result.

In just a moment, I will begin to describe for you the opening of the first seal, which ushers in the rule of the antichrist on earth. In Chapter Seven, I will talk about seals two through six. I will explain the seventh seal—which is a doozie, by the way—in Chapter Nine.

But before I begin to talk about the seven seals, let's take a quick look at the big picture. Why does this happen? What could possibly be the purpose behind the seals?

I believe that the purpose is twofold:

1) One reason is to bring wrath and judgment on the ungodly nations that have persecuted God's people and turned their backs on God. Indeed, in Daniel 3:21 (fifth letter, sixth word, ELS of 144) we find the name "Jesus," while adjacent letters at the same ELS spell "Son of God" and "Judge of the world."

2) A second reason for opening the seals and raining chaos and destruction onto the earth is to drive toward repentance the Nation of Israel so that she might be saved.

The Prophet Isaiah gives us a portrait of God's relationship with Israel and also God's plan for the final days. In six powerful verses, Isaiah gives us a look at the "big picture." He paints for us, in broad, sweeping strokes, a portrait of what has been and what is yet to come. Indeed, he weaves a tapestry of rich images that appear to not only describe the relationship—past and future—between Israel and God, but also describe God's victory over Satan in the final days. Using the imagery of Israel as a woman, this is what he has written:

Like as a woman with child, that draweth near the time of her delivery, is in pain, and crieth out in her pangs; so have we been in thy sight, O LORD. We have been with child, we have been in pain, we have as it were brought forth wind; we have not wrought any deliverance in the earth; neither have the inhabitants of the world fallen. Thy dead men shall live, together with my dead body shall they arise. Awake and sing, ye that dwell in dust: for thy dew is as the dew of herbs, and the earth shall cast out the dead.

Come, my people, enter thou into thy chambers, and shut thy doors about thee: hide thyself as it were for a little moment, until the indignation be overpast. For, behold, the LORD cometh out of his place to punish the inhabitants of the earth for the iniquity: the earth also shall disclose her blood, and shall no more cover her slain.

In that day the LORD with his sore and great and strong sword shall punish leviathan the piercing serpent, even leviathan that crooked serpent; and he shall slay the dragon that is in the sea.

(ISAIAH 26:17—27:1)

There are at least seven outstanding statements in the above verses that shed light on forthcoming events and the conclusion of this age:

A woman is having birth pangs. This woman represents Israel, striving in vain to give birth to new life. In this passage, she is in great pain—and, indeed, no one denies that the nation of Israel has suffered greatly through the years and in fact still suffers—yet she is unable to accomplish her goal. She delivers only wind, and not the child and life that she longs for. This is an interesting image considering the centuries that Israel has spent waiting in vain for the arrival of a Messiah who has, in fact, already come! I believe this verse also refers to the final stage of intense suffering that Israel will experience during the Tribulation as she cries out to be delivered from the horrendous culmination of centuries of persecution and rejection by the nations of the world.

The dead shall live; together with my dead body they shall rise. This references the bodily Resurrection of Christ and also foreshadows the resurrection of the saints at the time of the rapture.

Come, my people, enter into your chambers. I believe this is a picture of the rapture of the Church as believers are caught up to meet their Lord in the sky. We know that the word used here for "chambers" is the same as the Hebrew word for mansion, or the bridegroom's marriage room. We also know that the church is called the bride of Christ. In fact, Joel 2:16—a verse in which God's people are instructed to gather as a "bride" meeting her "bridegroom"—contains two important Bible codes. The first Bible code (first letter, eleventh word, ELS of -1) spells "Jesus" while the phrase "the glowing bride of God" is encoded nearby. The chambers or bridegroom's marriage room is where Christ will take His bride to escape the time of indignation. What kind of indignation? The Hebrew word that is used for indignation is the same as fury or tribulation. The bridegroom will hide the bride as God's fury is poured out on the earth in the final days.

The Lord comes out of His place to punish the inhabitants of the earth. As we've seen, Christ has already returned once to the clouds above the earth to draw His bride away to safety. Now, he comes a second time—this time actually setting foot on earth—to punish and to judge.

The Lord punishes the ungodly. He wields His sword, great and strong. This represents the battle of Armageddon when the Lord rescues Israel, once and for all, from her travails and suffering. The Church has already been raptured, but the nation of Israel—still laboring in vain—has been enduring the Tribulation on earth. Now she is rescued in a spectacular fashion that will leave her enemies dead and no question as to the Identity of the One who rescues her.

The earth will disclose her blood and will no more cover her slain. This will be the day of vengeance when the Lord destroys the armies that have amassed against Israel. This is an image of mass destruction so great that the earth cannot even contain its dead.

The fleeing serpent is destroyed. The serpent leviathan and the dragon referenced in Revelation are one and the same. It is Lucifer, and despite his efforts to escape, he will be defeated once and for all! In fact, numerous Bible codes provide commentary on the inevitable end of Lucifer. These include "For Satan shall be bitter [boiling mad]" (Daniel 12:1, third letter, twenty-fifth word, ELS of -150), "Satan shall be bitter" (Genesis 12:1, third letter, third word, ELS of -144) and even the powerful phrase "Lucifer shall lament his severing [destruction and cutting into pieces]!" (Daniel 12:1, third letter, second word, ELS of 52). And in Isaiah 19:16 (second letter, eleventh word, ELS of -167) we find this victorious commentary: "to utterly destroy the antichrist, to sweep away."

What is the "big picture"? What exactly are God's purposes and intentions during the final days? I believe they are fourfold:

- To hide the Church in safety from His wrath
- To allow Israel to endure the final stages of labor and suffering before rescuing her for eternity
- To punish those who have not called upon His name
- And to defeat Satan and his minions once and for all

As we return to the seven seals, we will see how the opening of these seals—and the destruction and chaos that are, as a result, unleashed on earth—play a major role in how God accomplishes these goals.

Jesus Opens the First Seal: The Antichrist Is Revealed

Join me as we return to John's vision and see what is happening in Heaven. The last we knew, John was weeping because there was no one worthy to open the seals when suddenly Jesus, as a Slain Lamb, steps forward to do the job.

What happens when Jesus breaks the first seal? John writes:

"And I saw when the Lamb opened one of the seals, and I heard, as it were the noise of thunder, one of the four beasts saying, Come and see. And I saw, and behold a white horse: and he that sat on him had a bow; and a crown was given unto him: and he went forth conquering, and to conquer" (Revelation 6:1–2).

It is generally accepted by theologians and scholars that the man on the white horse is the antichrist, also referred to in Revelation 13 as "the beast out of the sea."

The Bible certainly has much to say about the antichrist. In fact, the antichrist is mentioned many times throughout the Bible and by many names. These include the Assyrian, the king of Babylon, the spoiler, the extortioner, a king of fierce countenance, a prince that shall come, King of the north, the man of sin, the son of perdition, the wicked one, the beast, the cruel one, he who calls himself God, the little horn, a stern-faced king, the ruler who will come, the man of lawlessness, the man doomed to destruction and the beast coming out of the sea!

In addition, Bible codes have much to say about the antichrist as well. Here are a few examples: In the twenty-sixth chapter of Numbers we find, at 145 ELS, the phrase "shall be the president of the world." Adjacent letters at the same ELS tell us who shall be president of the world: "the serpent beast."

Encoded in the twenty-second chapter of Jeremiah, we find these phrases, each at an ELS of 41: "Lucifer is his name," "enemy," "one that does evil," "serpent," "the great lawlessness."

In the same chapter of Jeremiah, we find other phrases at a variety of other ELS numbers. For example, we find the phrase "wicked liar," as well as other references to this man as a beast or beast from the sea: "sea serpent," "leviathan," "the beast" and the places he comes from: "hell" and "the pit."

Encoded in the second chapter of Zechariah are the actual words "the antichrist," while if you begin with the third letter of the ninth word of Isaiah 35:15 and count forward every 261st letter, you will find the phrase "the deadly insult of the false prophet of his fury." Adjacent letters at the same ELS spell the phrase "the prince of persecution."

I think the following example is particularly fascinating because the encoded phrase so aptly reflects the message of the surface text.

Daniel 7:7 says: "After this I saw in the night visions, and behold a fourth beast, dreadful and terrible, and strong exceedingly; and it had great iron teeth: it devoured and brake in pieces, and stamped the residue with the feet of it: and it was diverse from all the beasts that were before it, and it had ten horns."

Who is this beast? If you start with the fifth letter of the twentieth word, then count forward every twenty-first letter, you will find the Hebrew letters that, translated, spell "the voice of the liar."

The Identity of the Antichrist

A t this time, we can only speculate as to who this man will be. Many Bible scholars believe that the antichrist will be a Jewish man. Coming from the previously conquered territory of the Roman Empire—perhaps from the Middle East—he will possess close ties with Israel, the European Union and Rome. One theory is that Israel will receive him as her long-awaited Messiah.

Revelation 13:18 gives us one cryptic clue as to the identity of this man: "Here is wisdom. Let him who has understanding calculate the number of the beast, for it is the number of a man: His number is 666." This number has even been discovered in Bible codes referring to the antichrist, while other codes refer to his lineage through the Roman empire: in 2 Chronicles 5:14, at an ELS of 81, is encoded the phrase "the savage mark of the Roman," while Daniel 12:10 contains the vivid code "the boasting, Roman beast" (first letter, twelfth word, ELS of -13).

Through the years, Bible scholars have tried to numerically identify the antichrist, checking the names of contemporary world figures to see if any of their names contain a numeric value of 666. (Using this kind of formula, one group has proven that the words "purple dinosaur" contain a numeric value of 666, thus concluding that the antichrist is none other than Barney!) Others have tried to discern the identity of this man by evaluating the characteristics of infamous individuals who seem to possess traits similar to those of the antichrist.

The bottom line is that we don't know for sure who this man will turn out to be, but we do know that when he is revealed, he will come in the name of peace, and he will possess a dynamic personality that will seduce the world. He will be recognized and even worshipped by the entire world, and—at least for a season of time—he will be allowed by God to wield great power and authority.

The Power Behind the Antichrist

Daniel 8:24 has this to say about the antichrist: "And his power shall be mighty, but not by his own power."

John goes into greater detail, telling us exactly who is providing power and authority to the antichrist: "And then I stood on the sand of the sea, and saw a beast rise up out of the sea, having seven heads and ten horns, and upon his horns ten crowns, and on his heads the name of blasphemy. . . . And the dragon [Satan] gave him his power, and his seat, and great authority" (Revelation 13:1–2).

What will he do with the power afforded him by Satan?

Daniel 8:24 tells us: "He shall destroy wonderfully, and shall prosper, and practise, and shall destroy the mighty and the holy people."

John, seeing scenes from the future, writes:

And I saw one of his heads as it were wounded to death; and his deadly wound was healed: and all the world wondered after the beast. And they worshipped the dragon which gave power unto the beast: and they worshipped the beast, saying, Who is like unto the beast? who is able to make war with him? And there was given unto him a mouth speaking great things and blasphemies; and power was given unto him to continue forty and two months. And he opened his mouth in blasphemy against God, to blaspheme his name, and his tabernacle, and them that dwell in heaven. And it was given unto him to make war with the saints, and to overcome them: and power was given him over all kindreds, and tongues, and nations.

(REVELATION 13:3–7)

In other words, the Bible tells us that the antichrist will use his power to blaspheme God, persecute Israel, and make war with the saints who receive Christ during the Tribulation!

The Antichrist's Treaty with Israel

Many believe that the antichrist will be well trained and brilliant in the arts of persuasion and that he will ooze with charisma and charm. In other words, this man will look good. He will look so good, in fact, that he will convince many Jews that he is the long-awaited Messiah. He will perform many deceptions—with Satan's assistance, of course—even appearing to raise someone from the dead!

But one of the most significant things that this man will accomplish is described in the ninth chapter of Daniel where we read the following words:

"And . . . the prince that shall come . . . shall confirm the covenant with many for one week . . ." (Daniel 9:26–27). The word "many" here refers to the nation of Israel, while the word "week" doesn't refer to an actual seven-day week, but to a period of seven years.

I like the way it is worded in the New Living Translation: "A ruler will arise [who] . . . will make a treaty with the people for a period of one set of seven."

This is widely accepted to be referring to a seven-year treaty with Israel. In other words, the antichrist will come on the scene and accomplish what no leader before him has been able to do: bring peace to the strife-torn Middle East! No wonder the world will sit up and take notice! No wonder many will hail him as the Messiah! No wonder his charisma and skills will elicit the adoration and even worship from the nations of the world!

But let's not be fooled for a single minute. A passage in 2 Thessalonians gives us a vivid picture of the character and intentions of this man:

"Let no man deceive you by any means: for that day [the day that Christ returns to earth in victory] shall not come, except there be a falling away first, and that man of sin is revealed, the son of perdition. . . ."

Did you pay attention to the powerful words used to describe the character of this man? He is called "the man of sin" and "the son of perdition." Perdition is a word we don't really use today, but it means "loss of the soul," "eternal damnation" and even "utter ruin."

2 Thessalonians goes on to say that this man is someone "who opposeth and exalteth himself above all that is called God, or that is worshipped, so that he as God sitteth in the temple of God, shewing himself that he is God."

Indeed, in the next several chapters, we will see that this is exactly what he does. Remember, this man is not operating in his own power, but under the influence and authority of none other than Satan himself. We will pick up on his story in Chapter Eight, but until then let me just say that he will not only break the peace treaty with Israel, but he will also desecrate the Holy Temple, demand to be worshipped as a god, and persecute Jews and Tribulation saints even unto death!

Right now, God is holding back the revelation of the antichrist. But as we are told in 2 Thessalonians 2:7, "For the mystery of iniquity doth already work; only he who now letteth will let, until he be taken out of the way." In other words, the wheels are in motion. I personally believe that the antichrist is alive and waiting for circumstances to fall into place that will enable his rapid rise. Perhaps he is a young man, or perhaps he is already well-versed in the arts of persuasion, lurking in the wings of the stage of world politics, waiting for the events that will illuminate his path to power.

There is good news, however! Let's look at the rest of 2 Thessalonians 2:8: "And then shall that Wicked [the antichrist] be revealed, whom the Lord shall consume with the spirit of His mouth, and shall destroy with the brightness of his coming."

Even though the antichrist will wreak havoc on the world for a season, in the end, he will be consumed by the mere breath—and destroyed by the brightness—of our Lord Jesus Christ!

This is such a comforting truth to hold in our hearts, particularly as we continue in our study of the rest of the seals. What we must always remember is this: God is the One restraining evil in the world, He is the One who can and will unleash fury and judgment, and He is the One who will crush Satan once and for all.

Yesterday, today and tomorrow . . . God is in charge!

SEVEN

Warnings Before Wrath:
The Tribulation Begins

From the moment the antichrist signs a treaty with Israel, the clock begins ticking! We can think of it as a Tribulation Countdown of sorts, because from the moment the antichrist signs the treaty with Israel, only seven years remain until Jesus returns, in full splendor, to win the Battle of Armageddon, redeem the Nation of Israel and put an end to Satan's power forever!

And what years these are! These seven years are what are commonly referred to as the Tribulation, and the most amazing, terrible things happen within these eighty-four months. Indeed, Bible codes refer to "the snare of the cruel one" (Daniel 2:30, fourth letter, twenty-second word, ELS of -38) and the "day of the angry fool" (Isaiah 45:9, second letter, fifteenth word, ELS of -41).

As we shall see, the countdown begins as Jesus, the Lamb of God, continues opening the second, third, fourth, fifth and sixth seals securing the scroll that He alone is worthy to receive from the right hand of God. As He breaks the seals, wars, famine, death, bloodshed, earthquakes and meteors are unleashed on earth to plague and judge the wicked. And because people often cry out to God when they face chaos and suffering, we also see that God is using these disasters to set the stage for one final chance at repentance for the Nation of Israel and anyone else who will listen. Indeed, even as God is punishing the wicked, seals one through six don't represent the worst of God's wrath as much as they represent severe warnings. The message is this: "The full fury of God's wrath will soon be delivered—so repent now and turn to Him!"

Let's take a closer look at God's severe warnings as the Lamb breaks the next five seals.

Jesus Opens the Second Seal: Nations Go to War

The first seal, as we saw in Chapter Six, heralded the arrival of a white horse bearing the antichrist. Seals two, three and four bring three other horses and riders. These are commonly referred to as "the four horsemen of the Apocalypse." Does God actually unleash four spiritual beings who then goad into existence various conditions on earth, or do these horsemen merely represent certain conditions and horrors that begin to take place on earth? I can't say for sure, and perhaps it doesn't matter. What matters is that, as a result of the opening of these first four seals, evil, war, famine and death prevail!

Here is what John wrote specifically about the second seal: "And when he had opened the second seal, I heard the second [living creature] say, Come and see. And there went out another horse that was red: and power was given to him that sat thereon to take peace from the earth, and that they should kill one another: and there was given unto him a great sword" (Revelation 6:3–4).

The rider of the red horse stampedes onto the scene bringing war to the world. He has been given a sword and the ability to "take peace from the earth."

Many scholars believe that war will engulf the world as a trio of nations see through the façade of the antichrist and take action to revolt against his rule. Even though Scripture indicates that they will not be successful at freeing themselves from his tyranny, they *will* manage to launch a very bloody world war!

Wartime today has some particularly frightening implications. Because of the availability of biological and nuclear warheads, all-out war can produce serious ramifications in terms of disease, plagues and viruses as well as mass destruction to both human life and to the ecology of our planet!

It makes sense that, in the wake of the kind of power-driven hatred and killing described in these verses, there would be ramifications in the world economy as well as a massive death toll. Indeed, we see, by the names and natures of the next two horsemen, that this is precisely what occurs.

Jesus Opens the Third Seal: Famine Sweeps the Earth

Revelation 6:5–6 tells us: "And when he had opened the third seal, I heard the third [living creature] say, Come and see. And I beheld, and lo a black horse; and he that sat on him had a pair of balances in his hand. And I heard a voice in the midst of the four [living creatures] say, A measure of wheat for a penny, and three measures of barley for a penny; and see thou hurt not the oil and the wine."

Famine often follows war, and here we see the black horseman, representing famine, appear on earth. The balances in his hand indicate scarcity of food, and the reference to a measure of wheat for a penny indicates that it will cost a day's wages to purchase supplies for a day's living.

As is often the case, the rich will not feel the effects of the famine as harshly as the poor. We know this happens because, in John's vision, he hears the instruction to "hurt not the oil and the wine." This famine will exact its toll predominantly on the middle class and the poor.

Jesus Opens the Forth Seal: Death Is Rampant

As Jesus opens the fourth seal, John hears the fourth beast say, "Come and see." John writes, "And I looked, and behold a pale horse: and his name that sat on him was Death, and Hell followed with him. And power was given unto them over the fourth part of the earth, to kill with sword, and with hunger, and with death, and with the beasts of the earth" (Revelation 6:7–8).

What a horrifying pronouncement!

Swords, hunger and death need little explanation. But beasts of the earth? So many of us live in urban and suburban cities where the wildest beasts in town are subject to leash laws and wear flea collars to boot! It appears that we would have little to fear from beasts of the earth!

There are, however, organisms on earth that have the power to kill and destroy at any address, be it in the jungles of South America or a highrise in New York.

Indeed, many scholars believe that this verse may be referring to unprecedented outbreaks of viruses and other organic killers. In fact, it is clear that, during the Tribulation, all manner of incurable diseases, plagues, and deadly viruses will reach pandemic levels and will surpass the worst epidemics in history.

Bible codes refer to at least two organic killers that will play a deadly role during the Tribulation: anthrax and cholera!

You and I have already seen the terrifying effects of anthrax. It has been used by terrorists in the past and will be used again during the Tribulation. Referred to as "burning coal" in Webster's Encyclopedia, anthrax produces ulcers on the skin—hot black blisters—caused by a bacillus that is highly infectious.

In Genesis 41:9, if you go to the fourth letter of the eleventh word, then count forward every ninety-fourth letter, you will find the phrase "anthrax death." The adjacent letters at the same ELS spell "sickness." In Daniel 5:11, begin with the sixth letter in the twelfth word, then count forward every eighty-seventh letter and you will find the phrase "the misty spread of anthrax." Adjacent letters at the same ELS spell "blisters of fire" and "the defected bacillus." "Defected" means that this deadly virus has been tampered with—in other words, it has been genetically engineered.

Regardless of the exact nature of virus or bacterium, it is clear that the plague will claim many lives. Start with Daniel 12:6, the fourth letter of the second word, and count backward seven letters at a time and you will find the phrase "skin disease." In the very next verse of Daniel, start with the third letter of the eighth word and count forward every twenty-eight letters and you will find the phrase "shall be disease" while "pestilence, waste" and "shall be the heights of pestilences" are found in Daniel 12:4 and in 2:9.

As already mentioned, the rider of the pale horse brings death. It is interesting to note that the Greek word for *pale* is *choloros*. This

ותא‎ח‎ריהן‎ותבל‎ל‎ענההשבלי‎י‎סהדק‎ותאתשבעההשבל
אאתכלחרטמימצריםואתכלחכמיהויספרפרעהל
כירהיו‎ס‎פרעהקצףעלעבדיווייתןאתיבמשמרבי
וחלמנו‎ו‎שמאתנוונערעברי‎עבדלשרהטבחהימסונס
לכנ‎י‎ואת‎ו‎תל‎ל‎הויישל‎ח‎פרעהויקראאתיוספ‎ו‎ירי
ופתראי‎ז‎אתוואנישמעתיעלידלאמרתשמעמחלום
לי‎ו‎סף‎ב‎ח‎למיהננ‎יעמדעלשפתהיארוההנהמן‎ה‎יא
חריהזד‎ל‎ותורעותתארמאדורקותבשרלאראיתי
בריאת‎ו‎ה‎באנההאלקרבנהולאנודעכיבאואלקרב
תוטבותוהנהשבעעשבלים‎צנמותדקותשדפותקדי

○ Anthrax Death
□ Sickness

translates in Hebrew to *cholera,* a dreaded disease that has plagued mankind for centuries. Cholera is an intestinal disease, most commonly found in India and other Asiatic countries. It is caused by a bacterium that is very contagious. The bacteria attacks the walls of the intestines, poisoning the system. Symptoms include severe diarrhea and intense vomiting, resulting in shock and death.

The Hebrew word for *cholera* is encoded in Daniel 2:24 at five-letter intervals. What is even more interesting is the fact that this particular reference to cholera is encoded in the passage of scripture in which Daniel interprets Nebuchadnezzar's prophetic dream foretelling of the last days.

The Hebrew word for *cholera* is encoded another time in the Old Testament, this time in Jeremiah 42:22: start with the first letter in the eleventh word, then count forward every twenty-second letter and you will find the word *cholera.* To find this word encoded in this passage is particularly mind-blowing because much in this chapter mirrors what we have just seen and read in Revelation! This chapter records a time when Israel—once again—refuses to obey the commandments of the Lord. In response, the Lord has Jeremiah give the following message to Israel: "And now I have this day declared it to you; but ye have not obeyed the voice of the Lord your God, nor any thing for the which he hath sent me unto you. Now therefore know certainly that ye shall die by the sword, by the famine, and by the pestilence. . . ." And in the middle of these dire words is encoded the word *cholera*!

Consider the eerie similarities between this verse (and its encoded message) and Revelation 6:7–8 when God punishes an unrepentant and rebellious world by unleashing a pale or *choloros* rider with the power to kill "with sword, and with hunger, and with death, and with the beasts of the earth."

Coincidence? Far from it! And yet the details remain sketchy at best. What we *do* know without a shadow of doubt, however, is that the rider of the pale horse brings death to earth. In fact, by the time the rider of the pale horse exacts his toll, one fourth of the world's population will have died as a result of wars, famines, governmental controls and the diabolical influences of the antichrist. Based on the population of the world today, that would be one billion people! Imagine the emotional and logistical chaos that will ensue! One fourth of the world's population will have died within twenty-one months. I can't imagine the kind of grief that will sweep the nations—not to mention the nightmare challenge of disposing of the remains of more than a billion people.

At this point, life on earth has changed completely and forever. The Rapture took one third of the world's population in the twinkling of an eye, then within twenty-one months, one fourth of the remaining population will have died prematurely due to supernatural and man-made disaster.

And yet the horrors continue!

Jesus Opens the Fifth Seal: Persecution Prevails

John writes: "And when he had opened the fifth seal, I saw under the altar the souls of them that were slain for the word of God, and for the testimony which they held: And they cried with a loud voice, saying, How long, O Lord, holy and true, dost thou not judge and avenge our blood on them that dwell on the earth? And white robes were given unto every one of them; and it was said unto them, that they should rest yet for a little season, until their fellow servants also and their brethren, that should be killed as they were, should be fulfilled" (Revelation 6:9–11).

Many scholars believe that a season before the rapture, but certainly during the Tribulation period, a great revival will spread across the world. Indeed, we shall see that—as geological, economic and political conditions on earth continue to deteriorate— God is still in the business of drawing people to Himself. A prophetic passage from the second chapter of Joel describes this revival of God's chosen people just before and during the early years of the Tribulation:

And it shall come to pass afterward, that I will pour out my spirit upon all flesh; and your sons and your daughters shall prophesy, your old men shall dream dreams, your young men shall see visions: And also upon the servants and upon the handmaids in those days will I pour out my spirit. And I will shew wonders in the heavens and in the earth, blood, and fire, and pillars of smoke. The sun shall be turned into darkness, and the moon into blood, before the great and the terrible day of the Lord come. And it shall come to pass, that whosoever shall call on the name of the Lord shall be delivered: for in mount Zion and in Jerusalem shall be deliverance, as the Lord hath said, and in the remnant whom the Lord shall call.

(JOEL 2:28–32)

God's Spirit outpoured! Prophecies! Dreams! Visions! A remnant called and delivered in the midst of great and terrible tribulations! I believe that four things will help set the stage for this "last days" move of God's Holy Spirit upon the earth.

For starters, many of those who are left behind will recognize the rapture for what it is, realizing they have been left behind to face the time of Tribulation. They will also recognize the antichrist for who he is—a deceiver and counterfeiter. Others will remember what they once learned about God in Sunday School or on TV, or read in a book or tract. Many of these individuals will now accept Christ as their Savior and Messiah.

Second, there will be those who will cry out to God—not because of any prior training they received as children or adults—but simply because of the magnitude of suffering that will be wrought upon the earth.

Third, the Bible tells us that Jesus is going to gather 144,000 individuals from the nation of Israel who believe that Jesus is the Christ. God seals and protects these Jewish believers with His Holy Spirit, and they boldly preach the Gospel to anyone who will listen.

Fourth, He sends two prophets back to earth—the Bible calls them the "two witnesses"—who travel, do miracles and preach the Gospel. As men and women hear the message of the two witnesses and also of the 144,000 Jews, many will accept Jesus Christ as their savior, refuse to worship the antichrist, and will be killed by beheading and other means for their faith. We will learn more about these two witnesses in Chapter Eight, but until then let me just say that, because of the evangelistic efforts of these two individuals as well as that of the 144,000, many will call on the name of Jesus Christ.

Tragically, those who follow Christ during these years—often called "Tribulation Saints"—will do so at a great price. This is because, during the Tribulation, Christians will experience the most severe persecution the world has ever known. The Bible tells us that anyone who accepts Jesus Christ will be killed and their blood will cry out from the grave! Revelation 6:11 gives us the tragic picture of these martyred souls being given white robes and instructions to rest a little while longer beneath the altar at the throne of God until all is fulfilled. More Christians are yet to be martyred before it is finally over.

Jesus Opens the Sixth Seal: God's Wrath Is Revealed

And I beheld when he had opened the sixth seal, and, lo, there was a great earthquake; and the sun became black as sackcloth of hair, and the moon became as blood. And the stars of heaven fell unto the earth, even as a fig tree drops her untimely figs, when she is shaken of a mighty wind. And the heaven departed as a scroll when it is rolled together, and every mountain and island were moved out of their places. And the kings of the earth, and the great men, and the rich men, and the chief captains, and the mighty men, and every bondman, and every free man, hid themselves in the dens and in the rocks of the mountains; And said to the mountains and rocks, Fall on us, and hide us from the face of him who sits on the throne, and from the wrath of the Lamb! For the great day of His wrath has come, and who shall be able to stand?

(REVELATION 6:12–17)

Merciful God! Talk about all hell breaking loose!

As this sixth seal is opened, we begin to see the fury of God's wrath unfold as he responds to the brutal slaying of the Tribulation Saints, and also centuries of rebellion and wickedness on earth. The Lamb opens the sixth seal and a massive earthquake rocks the world, triggering volcanic eruptions that cause the sun to be blocked and the moon to appear red like blood.

The concept of a catastrophic event occurring in such a way that the sun is darkened and the moon turns red is not unheard of. Indeed, geologists have determined that precisely this kind of event occurred sometime between A.D. 100 and A.D. 1200.

They believe the culprit was a volcano on Krakatoa, one of the islands of Indonesia. As a result of this volcanic eruption, two thirds of the island of Krakatoa collapsed into the sea, splitting what was left into three islands and generating a series of devastating tidal waves that pounded coastlines as far as 7,000 miles and left more than 36,000 people dead. The eruption was heard 3,000 miles away and spewed so much volcanic ash into the atmosphere that it hid the sun and turned the moon a blood red for 150 miles in every direction.

When we consider the devastating impact of this one volcanic explosion, we realize that the horrors described in the Bible aren't far-fetched at all. Could God's wrath unleash massive volcanic activity capable of darkening the sun, bloodying the moon and rocking all the mountains and islands? Absolutely!

In addition to all that I've just described, the Bible tells us that the stars of heaven—meteors—will fall to the earth. Let me assure you that what is being described here is a far cry from the child's game of wishing on a falling star!

What kind of destruction and catastrophe can be created by a single meteor?

At 7:17 A.M. on June 30, 1908, a mysterious explosion occurred in the skies over Siberia. It was caused by the impact and breakup of a large meteorite in the atmosphere.

Russian scientists collected eyewitness accounts of the event. Observers reported mighty explosions and a fiery cloud on the horizon. The object was seen in the cloudless sky as a brilliant, sun-like fireball. The closest observers were some reindeer herders asleep in their tents. The impact of the meteor crashing into our atmosphere created such force that these men were blown into the air and knocked unconscious; one man was hurled into a tree and later died.

Here is what one witness said about the meteor:

I was sitting on the porch of the house at the trading station, looking north. Suddenly in the north . . . the sky was split in two, and high above the forest the whole northern part of the sky appeared covered with fire. I felt a great heat, as if my shirt had caught fire. . . . At that moment there was a [deafening explosion] and a mighty crash. . . . I was thrown twenty feet from the porch and lost consciousness for a moment. . . . The crash was followed by a noise like stones falling from the sky, or guns firing. The earth trembled. . . . At the moment when the sky opened, a hot wind, as if from a cannon, blew past the huts from the north.

Another witness described the sky opening like a zipper and fire pouring out of the rip before the sky closed again. As I read his words, I couldn't help but remember John's words from Revelation 6:13–14: "And the stars of heaven fell unto the earth . . . and the heaven departed as a scroll when it is rolled together"! Here is what this witness had to say:

> *I saw the sky in the north open to the ground and fire poured out. The fire was brighter than the sun. We were terrified, but the sky closed again and immediately afterward, bangs like gunshots were heard. We thought stones were falling. . . . I ran with my head down and covered, because I was afraid stones may fall on it.*

For ten miles from the point where the meteor ripped into Earth's atmosphere, trees were blown over from the blast. Herders camped in tents about thirty miles away reported:

> *Early in the morning when everyone was asleep in the tent, it was blown up in the air along with its occupants. Some lost consciousness. When they regained consciousness, they heard a great deal of noise and saw the forest burning around them, much of it devastated. The ground shook and incredibly prolonged roaring was heard. Everything round about was shrouded in smoke and fog from burning, falling trees. Eventually the noise died away and the wind dropped, but the forest went on burning.*

All of this occurred as the result of a single meteor! Imagine the catastrophe and destruction that would ensue if the sky dropped meteors in the same fashion as a fig tree sheds its overripe fruit, as the Bible tells us will occur! The Bible tells us that men and women will literally run for the hills seeking safety and shelter!

The Bible is clear that, as God demonstrates his fury, conditions on earth will deteriorate to the point where every person—rich or poor, influential or derelict—will discover himself in the same destitute predicament. People from every walk of life will take to the hills seeking safety, crying out to the mountains and rocks, "Fall on us, and hide us from the face of Him that sitteth on the throne, and from the wrath of the Lamb." Notice that when catastrophe strikes, these rebellious people do not turn to God for help. Instead, they try to hide from God! Even threatened by death and eternal damnation, these people refuse to acknowledge God as God! Even Bible codes provide commentary on the stubborn wickedness of those reaping the bitter fruit of God's wrath: Exodus 21:18 (second letter, eighth word, ELS of 188) spells "the rebellious man," while Psalm 14:5 contains a code at an ELS of 15 that spells "the foolish people," and in Isaiah 45:9 we find two Bible codes: "the atheist shall be a thorn" and "day of the angry fool"!

What would it be like to be threatened with destruction so horrible that masses seek safety in the rocks, mountains and hills? Once again, history provides us with a heartrending portrait of just such an event. Even though the volcanic eruption on the island of Krakatoa occurred an unknown number of years ago, in 1883 writings were discovered that contained eyewitness reports of the devastation of that unfathomable catastrophe.

One of the most harrowing accounts of this event came from a field hand working in an inland paddy field on Java. Here is his shocking description of a brutal scenario of "survival of the fittest" as men and women flee to the hills and rocks, seeking safety from certain death as they are threatened by a wall of sea water:

All of a sudden there came a great noise. We . . . saw a great black thing, a long way off, coming towards us. It was very high and very strong, and we soon saw that it was water. Trees and houses were washed away. . . . The people began to . . . run for their lives. Not far off was some steep sloping ground. We all ran towards it and tried to climb up out of the way of the water. The wave was too quick for most of them, and many were drowned almost at my side. . . . There was a general rush to climb up in one particular place. This caused a great block, and many of them got wedged together and could not move. Then they struggled and fought, screaming and crying out all the time. Those below tried to make those above them move on again by biting their heels. A great struggle took place for a few moments, but . . . one after another, they were washed down and carried far away by the rushing waters.

There is one more seal, and it is a shocker! If you think the world and mankind have groaned and suffered under the influence of seals one through six, wait until you see what happens when The Lamb breaks the final seal and God's great and terrible wrath bears its final horror of horrors!

We'll pick up on the seventh seal in a later chapter. Until then, let's take a look at a few of the Bible's many encoded messages that shed light on the things we've just been discussing.

Bible Codes Paint a Grisly Picture

T he twelfth chapter of Daniel brims with codes that describe many of the things we've just been talking about. With references to disease, famine, earthquakes, floods, calamity, meteors, violence, demons and even the antichrist, Bible codes in this chapter present a chilling commentary on the last days.

Here are a few of the codes offering frightening insights:

Encoded in the text of only seven verses—Daniel 12:3 through 12:10—these phrases can be found: "shall be severe famine," "drought," "shall be meteors," "hail shall afflict," "shall be earthquakes," "bitter earthquakes," "shall be angry floods."

We have also discovered references to man's wickedness and love of violence. Begin with the first letter of the eighth word of Daniel 12:1 and count forward forty letters at a time, and you will find the phrase "time of rebellion." Three verses later, in Daniel 12:4, begin with the first letter of the tenth word and count forward every seventy-four letters and you will find the phrase "you shall commit loathsome murder." Two verses later is encoded the phrase "shall be many crimes" while "drugs, calamity" is found in the very next verse. In Daniel 12:8 we find the phrase "man will be in great distress" while "daily violences" appears in Daniel 12:12.

Believe it or not, this same chapter also contains numerous fascinating encoded references to technology! Start with the second letter of the twenty-first word of Daniel 12:1 and count forward every fifty-one letters and you will find "the car." This same verse—beginning with the fifth letter of the seventeenth word and counting forward fourteen letters at a time—contains the word "train." The phrase "shall be electricity" also appears in this same verse: you can find it by beginning with the third letter of the twenty-third word, then counting backward at an ELS of 151. A few verses later—first letter of the thirteenth word of Daniel 12:4, count backward at an ELS of 13—you can find "the light appointed for their fuel," a phrase that would appear to refer to solar energy!

The thought-provoking phrase "shall be spacecraft" isn't found in chapter twelve, but bears mentioning nevertheless. Go to the first letter of the thirteenth word of Daniel 11:37, count backward at an ELS of 19, and you will find this phrase.

"The day of knowledge" is found in Daniel 12:3, while "computer on line" has been discovered nearby in Daniel 12:6. "Telecommunication of God" begins in Daniel 12:4 (third letter of the fourth word, ELS of 49), while "broadcasting the light" (12:8, third letter, eighth word, ELS of 67) and "broadcasting transmitter" (12:11, second letter, sixth word, ELS of -5) and even the cryptic "the destructive telecommunication from the wicked" (Daniel 12:1; fifth letter fourth word, ELS of 65) are encoded nearby.

As a side note, let me mention that hidden codes don't provide the only reference to modern communications technology in the Bible. In the prophetic book of Zechariah we find this fascinating description of a vision in which Zechariah sees "a flying roll; the length thereof is twenty cubits, and the breadth thereof ten cubits." Charles Miller, in his book *Today's Technology in Bible Prophecy*, explains that

A roll was an ancient book in the form of a rolled manuscript, usually made of parchment. Ancient parchments were commonly called scrolls. . . . A rolled up scroll was cylindrical in shape and looked like a modern roll of paper towels. Rolls were communication devices that allowed men to send and receive information.

Although Zechariah had no idea what he was viewing at first glance, twentieth century people can make the connection between a flying roll and a modern communications satellite without difficulty.

Indeed, the dimensions of the "roll" that Zechariah saw in his vision equates to thirty feet long and fifteen feet in diameter—very similar dimensions to many of the communications satellites orbiting the earth even as I write this paragraph!

But returning to Bible codes, there is one last code in this fascinating cluster found in the twelfth chapter of Daniel that I would like to mention. It is the ominous phrase "evil scientific abortions of death." Imagine a controversial development in medical technology that delays death, not out of noble intentions, but for some evil intent! The stuff of science fiction? Perhaps—yet think of how many of today's modern conveniences were considered science fiction only a hundred years ago!

Hidden Codes and the Antichrist

Of all the messages encoded in the twelfth chapter of Daniel, the greatest number refer to Satan or the antichrist. I will detail many of these references for you in Chapter Eight. For now, let me tell you about one grouping of encoded messages that I find fascinating and revealing.

In Revelation 9:11, John writes: "And they had a king over them, which is the angel of the bottomless pit, whose name in the Hebrew tongue is Abaddon, but in the Greek tongue hath his name Apollyon." We don't know if Abaddon is Satan himself, the spirit of the antichrist, or another high-ranking demon. But whoever he is, he is the king of a horde of demonic tormentors—John describes them as locusts—who are given the power to harass and torment mankind for five months.

Fascinatingly enough, if you begin with the third letter in the first word of Daniel 12:6, then count forward every sixty-first letter, you will find the name "Abaddon." Adjacent letters at the same ELS spell "the demons." Nearby has been encoded the phrases "the treacherous pit," "the king of shame," and "the demon invasion"!

The fact is, during the Tribulation, Satan and the antichrist are having a field day. Given forty-two months to reign unhindered, Satan is alive and well on Planet Earth, and managing to wreak havoc, destruction and suffering in the process. Indeed, during the years of the Tribulation, "all hell breaks loose" as Satan rains suffering and even death onto the Tribulation Saints, curses God and demands to be worshipped.

As we are about to see in Chapter 8, Satan is the Beast and—at least for a season of time—the world is his lair.

EIGHT

In the Lair of the Beast

The last time we saw the antichrist, he had risen unexpectedly to great political power, confirmed a covenant with Israel and brought peace to a troubled world. But all has not been going well under his leadership.

At the beginning of his season of power, the antichrist will enjoy great popularity. Some scholars believe his popularity and political power will stem from the fact that he will appear to do the impossible in bringing peace to a strife-torn Middle East. Another theory is that he will capture the imagination and awe of a watching world when he appears to rediscover the Ark of the Covenant containing the stone tablets on which are written the Ten Commandments.

The Bible warns us that, for three and a half years, this man will speak out against God, His Kingdom as well as everyone in Heaven—

THE SHADOW OF THE APOCALYPSE

which I believe refers to all the people who were raptured just prior to the antichrist's rapid rise to power. He will also persecute the new Christians and overcome them. He is described as the "beast out of the sea" and Satan is described as "the dragon," and because of they worship the antichrist, people will worship Satan as well.

How does he amass so much power and authority? Let me talk for a moment about three factors that I believe lay the groundwork for his amazing hold on the affections of the world.

For one thing, signs and wonders are at work. In fact, it is clear that, at some point, the antichrist wins the awe of a watching world when he suffers a deadly head wound and yet heals and survives. Is this an assassination gone awry? We can only speculate. Here's what we know for sure: In Revelation 13:3, John sees an image of the antichrist as a beast with seven heads, then writes, "I saw one of his heads as if it were wounded to death, and his deadly wound was healed: and all the world wondered after the beast: and so they worshipped the dragon [Satan] which gave power unto the beast; and they worshipped the beast, saying, Who is like unto the beast? Who is able to make war with him?" A few verses later, in Revelation 13:14, John refers to the antichrist as "the beast, which had the wound by the sword, and did live."

What other seemingly supernatural factors contribute to his authority? Well, we already know the source of his authority and power. As we've discussed in Chapter Six, we know that the power of the antichrist "shall be great, but not by his own power" (Daniel 8:24) and that "the dragon," or Satan, is the one who gives him his power, throne and authority (Revelation 13:1). Even Bible codes appear to confirm the power source behind the beast. In Isaiah 24:18 is the encoded phrase "the evil Satan" (fifth letter, eleventh word, ELS of 38), while four verses later we find the encoded phrase "evil one in the beast" (Isaiah 24:22, fifth letter, eleventh word, ELS of 11).

Finally, during his years of influence, the antichrist will be joined by another presence. The Bible calls this new member of the cast by several names, including "the false prophet" and "the beast out of the earth." Whatever this man's role will be—vice president, spiritual counselor, political adviser—we know that he will lead the world to worship the antichrist and Satan as well, much like John the Baptist led people to worship Jesus Christ and God. In fact, the false prophet will create amazing signs, wonders and deceptions in order to accomplish his goal.

This is what John wrote about this second man, his mission, and some of the signs, wonders and deceptions he creates:

And I beheld another beast coming up out of the earth; and he had two horns like a lamb, and he spake as a dragon. And he exerciseth all the power of the first beast before him, and causeth the earth and them which dwell therein to worship the first beast, whose deadly wound was healed. And he doeth great wonders, so that he maketh fire come down from heaven on the earth in the sight of men, And deceiveth them that dwell on the earth by the means of those miracles which he had power to do in the sight of the beast; saying to them that dwell on the earth, that they should make an image to the beast, which had the wound by a sword, and did live. And he had the power to give life unto

the image of the beast, that the image of the beast should both speak,
and cause that as many as would not worship the image of the beast
should be killed.

(REVELATION 13:11–15)

What an intriguing description! It appears that this man creates an image of the antichrist and animates it in some fashion so that it appears to talk and even breathe. Isaiah 29:5 appears to contain an encoded reference to this image when it says, "an idolatrous idol of the beast" (fourth letter, ninth word, ELS of -61). Will this image be generated by technology? Could it be a hologram of some sort? We don't know. What we *do* know is that this man makes it mandatory—upon punishment by death—for citizens of every nation to worship this image.

The Mark of the Beast

This man—this "false prophet"—also appears to be the mastermind behind the "mark of the beast," a concept that has generated both fear and speculation for centuries.

Here is what John wrote about the mark:

And he causeth all, both small and great, rich and poor, free and bond,
to receive a mark in their right hand, or in their foreheads: And that no
man might buy or sell, save he that had the mark, or the name of the
beast, or the number of his name. Here is wisdom. Let him that hath

understanding count the number of the beast: for it is the number of a
man; and his number is Six hundred threescore and six.

(REVELATION 13:16—18)

Apparently some sort of identifying mark or symbol is created that represents, numerically, the name of the antichrist. What kind of mark will this be? We don't know for sure. What we *do* know is that once printed, tattooed or embedded in the forehead or hand, this mark becomes the "pass" that lets people buy or sell anything in this strange new world. Think of it as a PIN number or access code. More than a personal identification number, however, the mark will also be a *pledge* identification number that identifies whether or not you have pledged your allegiance to the antichrist.

A single identifying mark that will serve as your access code for every financial transaction you make? The stuff of science fiction? Hardly.

On May 20, 1998, in Washington, D.C., a subcommittee of the U.S. House of Representatives held a hearing. The topic of the hearing was "Biometrics and the Future of Money." The chairman presiding over the hearing was the Honorable Michael N. Castle. In a transcript of the hearing, Chairman Castle's opening remarks include the following comments:

Take a moment in your minds and add up all the passwords, PIN numbers, account numbers, voice mail access number and other security codes you have to deal with in your daily life. I would like to see a show of hands of those who have five or less [numbers] . . . to keep track of. . . . I see one hand out there. How many have five to ten? We are getting upward of maybe 40 or 50 percent [raising their hands]. How many poor souls have more than ten to manage? I think I am in that category. That is clearly in excess of 50 percent [raising their hands].

How many of you would cheerfully trade in all of these multi-digit codes if you could use one unique secure personal identifier for every purpose, one that was always at hand and could not be stolen, lost, forgotten or duplicated? Raise your hand if you are in that category. . . . about 100 percent in this case. . . . Trying to come up with that all-purpose or at least multi-purpose personal identifier is what the art and science of biometrics is all about.

During this particular hearing, expert witnesses talked about five possible technologies that could be used for such a purpose: facial recognition, finger imaging, iris scans, voice recognition and signature dynamics.

Whatever the means, the significance of the goal of this subcommittee can't be ignored! Their mission: to explore the development of a single PIN—for *everything*—that can't be lost, stolen or forged because it is a part of your own flesh. The wheels are already in motion to bring this kind of system into our daily lives. We possess the technology. What will be the catalyst that will finally thrust this kind of system upon us?

From our study of seals one through six, we already know that famine and economic hardship will be rampant. Will this "mark" be an attempt to ration limited resources? If so, perhaps it will be implemented after Jesus opens the third seal allowing widespread famine on the earth. If this is the case, however, why pervert a simple rationing program by using it to mandate idol worship?

Bible codes do not appear to be silent on the matter of the mark of the beast. In fact, a hidden message discovered encoded in Ezekiel 22:31 appears to speak to the ramification of refusing to accept this *pledge* identification number when it warns, "To pass over the mark for death" (ELS of 22).

Another encrypted message regarding the mark of the beast is found in Daniel 12:1: Begin with the second letter of the second word, count forward at an ELS of 29, and you will find the phrase "shall be the evil mark." Six verses later, beginning in Daniel 12:7, is encoded the phrase "the code-mark appointed." The phrase "mark of beast" is encoded in the text of Daniel 7:9.

Then, several chapters later, there appears to be encoded a stunning insight into the method used to implement the mark! Go to Daniel 9:26. Begin with the third letter in the second word, then count in reverse every five letters and you will find this commentary: "666 insert by incision."

Could the "mark" be inserted by incision? Could it be "worn" under the skin? You bet it could!

In fact, a company called Applied Digital Solutions (ADS) is currently marketing what they are calling a subdermal personal verification microchip. About the size of a grain of rice, the VeriChip is a tiny radio frequency identification device that is inserted under the skin. When read by a scanner, the dormant VeriChip becomes activated and transmits up to six lines of information. According to ADS, this information can be used for security, financial, emergency identification and healthcare applications.

Could this technology be used as a personal identification number of sorts, making it possible for financial transactions to take place? Absolutely. On his website, Richard M. Smith writes:

> *As a technologist, it is pretty clear to me that the VeriChip identification system can replace credit cards as a more convenient and secure method of paying for goods and services. . . . In commerce, I would expect for the VeriChip identification system to be used much as the SpeedPass system from ExxonMobil is used today: This system makes use of a key ring gadget to replace a credit card at self-service stations to buy gas. This system is now being expanded to McDonald's. In theory, it can work in any place of business that accepts credit cards and has a SpeedPass reader. A VeriChip payment system would work just like a SpeedPass, except a person would just wave their hand by a reader. I think that both consumers and merchants would find such a payment system very convenient to use.*

Once widely accepted as a personal identification number, could the VeriChip also be used as a *pledge* identification number, allowing only those men and women who have accepted the number—and thus pledged their allegiance to the antichrist—to engage in any financial transactions? Of course it could.

It's one thing for the VeriChip to exist on the drawing board or in some high-tech lab somewhere. But how eminent is its introduction into the mainstream of our everyday lives?

On May 10, 2002, Jeff Jacobs, his wife, Leslie, and their thirteen-year-old son Derek were embedded with VeriChips in their right arms. The family claimed that they wanted to "get chipped" for medical safety reasons—Jeff takes ten different medications, Leslie has a heart murmur, Derek has medicine allergies. In case any member of the Jacobs family ever shows up unconscious at a hospital, these facts can be read from the implanted chips.

The "chipping" of the Jacobs family has not gone without controversy.

At the time of the "chipping," there was debate as to whether the presence of medical information on the chip made the VeriChip a "medical device." This is an important distinction since the Food and Drug Administration initially approved the distribution of the chip as an identification device, not a medical device, which would have been required to pass much more rigorous scrutiny.

Some critics wrote that the Jacobses "chipping" was nothing short of a publicity stunt, since the VeriChips in their arms are useless unless a significant number of hospitals agree to purchase VeriChip scanners to activate the chips.

Individuals and politicians concerned with privacy issues are divided as to how the VeriChip will impact our privacy as individuals and consumers. Some people argue that the VeriChip will actually increase our privacy—after all, whatever information is accessible via chip is hidden from anyone who doesn't have a scanner, while anyone who glances at your driver's license immediately knows intimate details about your life, including your address and how much you weigh! Critics of the chip argue that anyone *with* a scanner can potentially get access to virtually any detail about your life!

Finally, both religious and secular media have commented on the VeriChip's obvious potential to serve the agenda of the antichrist and the "false prophet" as the mark of the beast. Some have predicted that the VeriChip will be a hard sell in the Christian marketplace because of the chip's potential for misuse and abuse by the antichrist. Indeed, concern over the chip's potential for abuse seems valid. According to ADS, the VeriChip could be combined with a global positioning system (GPS), which means that, via satellite, anyone with a chip could be tracked and located worldwide. The good news is that this kind of system could track and locate missing children, kidnapping victims, wandering Alzheimer's patients, convicted felons on parole, even terrorists—assuming that these individuals had been implanted at an earlier date with a biochip. In theory, could the VeriChip be used to track and locate people who embrace a faith or belief that has fallen out of political favor? Many experts fear that the answer to that question is "yes."

Despite these controversies and others, in the months following the televised "chipping" of the Jacobses, ADS reported receiving several thousand emails from teenagers who, like Derek, wanted to "get chipped." Indeed, at the time this book went to press, ADS appeared optimistic about the future of the VeriChip, having recently launched a national "Get Chipped" promotion aimed at attracting investors, establishing new authorized distribution centers and educating the public on the benefits of the VeriChip. At the time of this writing, ADS had already established seven authorized VeriChip centers in the cities of Phoenix, Arizona; San Antonio, Texas; Naples, Florida; Port St. Lucie, Florida; McLean, Virginia; Boca Raton, Florida; and Sunrise, Florida.

Will the VeriChip or a similar biochip play a role in the last-days agenda of the antichrist? Only time will tell. What is abundantly clear, however, is the fact that—daily—technology continues to line up neatly with what the Bible says about the last and final days!

The Abomination that
Desolates the Holy Temple

A s we are about to discover, a pivotal event during the reign of the antichrist takes place in Jerusalem, in the Temple. This might seem strange because, as you probably know, as I write these words there *is* no Jewish temple in Jerusalem. The Temple that once stood on the Temple Mount was burned to the ground nearly two thousand years ago, and today, on the Mount, sits the Dome of the Rock, the Muslim mosque that has been a focal point of Arab/ Israeli discord for generations.

Before I tell you exactly what event transpires in the Temple— and how it transpires in a temple that, at this moment, does not exist—let's take a quick look at some of the fascinating history of the Temple.

For starters, God revealed his plans for a Holy Temple to King David in a dream. After God told David *where* the Temple should be built and *how* it should be built, David rallied stoneworkers, black-smiths and lumbermen and began to purchase and prepare much of the materials that would be needed. But David, man of war that he was, was not commissioned to build the Temple himself.

In 1 Chronicles 22:6–10, we read:

Then [David] called for Solomon his son, and charged him to build an house for the Lord God of Israel. And David said to Solomon, My son, as for me, it was in my mind to build a house unto the name of the Lord my God: But the word of the Lord came to me, saying, Thou hast shed blood abundantly, and has made great wars: thou shalt not build a house unto my name, because thou hast shed much blood upon the earth in my sight. Behold, a son shall be born to thee, who shall be a man of rest; and I will give him rest from all his enemies round about: for his name shall be Solomon, and I will give peace and quietness unto Israel in his days. He shall build a house for my name.

I can imagine how disappointed David must have been that he would not get to build the Temple for which God had given him not just a passion, but the actual plans! And yet—I love this about David—he didn't wallow in disappointment or whine about the decision of his Lord. Instead, he passionately did everything he could to ensure the success of the man who *did* get to build the Temple! David invested his time and wealth to ready the materials and men for the privilege that was to belong to Solomon. Updating Solomon on everything that had already been done, David told his son:

Now, behold, in my trouble I have prepared for the house of the Lord a hundred thousand talents of gold, and a thousand thousand talents of silver; and of brass and iron without weight; . . . timber also and stone have I prepared; and thou mayest add thereto. Moreover there are workmen with thee in abundance, hewers and workers of stone and timber, and all manner of cunning men for every manner of work. Of the gold, the silver, and the brass, and the iron, there is no number. . . . Now set your heart and your soul to seek the Lord your God; arise therefore, and build ye the sanctuary of the Lord God, to bring the ark of the covenant of the Lord, and the holy vessels of God, into the house that is to be built to the name of the Lord.

(1 CHRONICLES 22:14—19)

Solomon did as his earthly father and his Heavenly Father commanded him to do. It took seven years and a work force of thirty thousand men, but Solomon did indeed build the house of the Lord. An extravagant compound—much of it overlaid with gold and adorned with precious stones—the Temple contained vessels, candlesticks, pillars, carvings and an elaborate altar, much of which was gold or brass, and crafted by the finest artisans of the times. Even the nails were made of gold! The Temple was completed in the year 960 B.C. and stood for 374 years until the tenth day of August in the year 586 B.C. That's the day that the Babylonians, led by King Nebuchadnezzar, leveled the Temple and carried the nation of Israel into captivity.

Seventy years later, the Medes and Persians, who had conquered Babylon, allowed the Jews to return to Jerusalem to rebuild their Temple. The second Temple was completed on March 12, 515 B.C.

A lot of significant events occurred in this rebuilt Temple. This is, after all, the Temple where—five hundred years later—Mary and Joseph arrived cradling their son and carrying two sacrificial doves so they could officially present their new baby to God. This is the place where Jesus, at twelve years old, became separated from His parents and was finally located sitting with the priests and teachers, wowing them with His wisdom. Roughly two decades later, Jesus was back at the Temple, furious with the "commercialization" of God's house and overturning the tables of vendors and money-changers.

The Temple is also the location where Jesus faced one of the three temptations presented to Him by Satan. After tempting Jesus—who had just fasted forty days and nights—Satan brings Jesus "home," to the house of His Father, and tempts Him to receive protection by taking advantage of His relationship with His Heavenly Father:

> And [Satan] brought him to Jerusalem, and set him on a pinnacle of the temple, and said unto him, If thou be the Son of God, cast thyself down from hence: For it is written, He shall give his angels charge over thee, to keep thee: And in their hands they shall bear thee up, lest at any time thou dash thy foot against a stone. And Jesus answering said unto him, It is said, Thou shalt not tempt the Lord thy God. And when the devil had ended all the temptation, he departed from him for a season.
> (LUKE 4:9–13)

In addition, we know from the gospels that Jesus spoke to the multitudes in and around the Temple, and it was at the Temple that Jesus addressed the scribes and Pharisees, calling them hypocrites, predators, blind guides, fools, tombs, serpents and vipers!

In fact, it was after communicating these very words to the religious leaders of His day that Jesus prophesied about the coming destruction of the Temple. In Matthew 24:1–2 we read: "And Jesus went out, and departed from the temple: and his disciples came to him for to show him the buildings of the temple. And Jesus said unto them, See ye not all these things? Verily I say unto you, There shall not be left here one stone upon another, that shall not be thrown down."

Indeed, it wasn't long after Jesus spoke those words—roughly forty years—that the Roman general Titus captured the city of Jerusalem. The year was A.D. 70, and after a grueling siege, the Temple was torched and burned on the tenth of August—the very day the Temple was burned to the ground by Nebuchadnezzar 656 years earlier.

The heat of the flames melted the mass quantities of gold adorning the temple, which turned molten and ran into the cracks of the stonework. Roman soldiers later pried the stones apart with their swords to get at the gold. As a result, no stones were left unturned, a vivid fulfillment of Jesus' words!

Nearly two thousand years have passed. Despite several thwarted attempts, the Temple has yet to be rebuilt. And with the Temple Mount currently occupied by a Muslim mosque and the focal point of bitter controversy, the third Temple remains a dream. This is despite the fact that there are numerous organizations and foundations—The Temple Institute (*www.templeinstitute.org*) being one of them—devoted to rallying scholars, architects, historians, funds, artisans and even descendents of the Levitical priesthood so that, when the time is right, the groundwork will be laid for the third Temple to be erected quickly.

God's house *will* be rebuilt. We know this because the rebuilt Temple plays a pivotal role in the last and final days.

In fact, the Temple *must* be rebuilt before the midpoint of the Tribulation. This is because, midway through the antichrist's seven-year treaty with Israel, he enters the Temple and does something so heinous that it breaks the treaty with Israel. Thus begins a three-and-a-half-year period that Jesus calls "the great tribulation." This is a time of intense suffering for the entire world and persecution unto death for anyone who professes a faith in Jesus Christ.

What exactly does the antichrist do in the Temple?

2 Thessalonians 2:4 tells us that the antichrist "will oppose and will exalt himself over everything that is called God, or that is worshipped; so that he as God sitteth in the temple of God, shewing himself that he is God."

He also apparently puts a halt to the Jewish ceremonies of worship taking place at the Temple, because in Daniel 12:11 we read that, 1,290 days before the end (that would be three and a half years before the end, placing this event at the midpoint of the Tribulation), the daily sacrifice is halted and something is put in its place that is not only an abomination, but that desolates the temple.

Jesus refers to this same event. When his disciples ask him, "What shall be the sign of thy coming, and of the end of the world?" he describes the very things we've been talking about throughout this book—wars, rumors of wars, famines, pestilences, earthquakes, persecution—and then talks about the event in the Temple that desolates the holy place and signals the beginning of "the great tribulation":

When ye therefore shall see the abomination of desolation, spoken of by
Daniel the prophet, stand in the holy place . . . then let them which be
in Judaea flee into the mountains: Let him which is on the housetop not
come down to take any thing out of his house: Neither let him which is
in the field return back to take his clothes. And woe unto them that are
with child, and to them that give suck in those days! But pray ye that
your flight be not in the winter, neither on the sabbath day: for then
shall be great tribulation, such as was not since the beginning of the
world to this time, no, nor ever shall be.

(MATTHEW 24:15–21)

What kind of "abomination" will stand in the holy place, signaling holy people to flee into the mountains? Many scholars believe
that this is where the "animated image" of the antichrist comes
into the picture. You'll remember the image as it is described in
Revelation 13:15: "And he [the false prophet] had power to give life
unto the image of the beast, that the image of the beast should both
speak, and cause that as many as would not worship the image of
the beast should be killed." Is this how the antichrist and false
prophet desolate the Holy Temple and abort the covenant they
confirmed with Israel? Many learned scholars would say yes. But
whatever the means, the Bible is clear on the bitter significance of
the antichrist's impact on the Holy Temple and on the lives of godly
people. Even Bible codes appear to confirm the heinous influence
of the antichrist. In Daniel 12:9, first letter of the ninth word and at
an ELS of 58, we find the phrase "destruction of the high place." A
few verses away, beginning at the third letter of the fourth word of
Daniel 12:4 (ELS of 41) the phrase "in the day of destruction, ter-

ror" has been discovered, while Daniel 12:3 (fifth letter, fifth word, ELS of -23) is the bloodcurdling statement "shall be an evil holocaust."

What Bible Codes Say about the Peace Treaty and the Nature of the Beast

In the fifth chapter of 2 Chronicles, we find a detailed description of the sacrifices, ceremonies and worship that accompanied the completion of the Holy Temple. Verses thirteen and fourteen give us this beautiful image of God's response to the praises of his people:

> It came even to pass, as the trumpeters and singers were as one, to make one sound to be heard in praising and thanking the Lord; and when they lifted up their voice with the trumpets and cymbals and instruments of music, and praised the Lord, saying, For he is good, for his mercy endureth for ever: that then the house was filled with a cloud, even the house of the Lord. So that the priests could not stand to minister by reason of the cloud: for the glory of the Lord had filled the house of God.

The beauty of these verses is starkly contrasted by the message of the Bible code that begins in verse fourteen and proceeds forward at an ELS of 35. The code refers to the antichrist's broken covenant with Israel, the aborted treaty that will culminate in the desolation of the rebuilt Holy Temple.

What does the code say? It says, "the bitter, seven-year charter." The adjacent letters—at the same ELS—spell "wars" and "the beast."

Daniel 8:19 and 25 provide another such example. The angel Gabriel comes to Daniel in a vision, saying, "Behold, I will make thee know what shall be in the last end."

Then, describing a king of fierce countenance—the antichrist—he says, "And through his policy also he shall cause craft to prosper in his hand; and he shall magnify himself in his heart, and by peace shall destroy many: he shall also stand up against the Prince of princes; but he shall be broken without hand." Beginning with the sixth letter of the eight word of this verse and counting in reverse at—once again!—an ELS of 35 (I find that interesting, don't you?), we find what appears to be a second reference to the antichrist's bitter convenant with Israel: "charter of the holocaust." In this same chapter, at the ELS of 81, we have found the phrase "the savage mark of the Roman."

And in the twelfth chapter of Daniel—the chapter in which Daniel describes his vision of the abomination that, once set up in the Holy Temple, not only stops the daily sacrifice to Jehovah but desolates the Temple—there exists a mind-boggling cluster of codes referring to the wicked motives of the antichrist's covenant with Israel.

Beginning in Daniel 12:5, go to the fourth letter in the third word, then count in reverse at an ELS of 88 and you will find the phrase "the adversary's treaty for all." Adjacent letters to this phrase—all at the same ELS of -88—further identify the being responsible for the treaty, as well as his evil intentions. The codes in this cluster that have been discovered so far include the following: "the beast," "his charter," "tribulation," "shall be from his evil covenant," "treaty," and "shall be his great trouble."

Two Witnesses

In the eleventh chapter of Revelation we find details of the ministry, death and resurrection of two individuals whom John calls "the two witnesses." Quoting the angel of the Lord, here's what John writes:

"And I will give power unto my two witnesses, and they shall prophesy a thousand two hundred and threescore days, clothed in sackcloth. . . . And if any man will hurt them, fire proceedeth out of their mouth, and devoureth their enemies: and if any man will hurt them, he must in this manner be killed."

So we know that these two men will minister under the protection of the Holy Spirit. While protected in this fashion, what will they seek to accomplish? Because they are called "witnesses" and "prophets," we can assume that they will be proclaiming the identity and agenda of their Holy God. In addition, John writes: "These have power to shut heaven, that it rain not in the days of their prophecy: and have power over waters to turn them to blood, and to smite the earth with all plagues, as often as they will."

As you can imagine, their message as well as their method of delivering that message will not render them particularly popular with the antichrist and any who follow him! And yet, protected for roughly three and a half years, these two individuals will speak out boldly for the cause of Christ.

After 1,260 days, their ministry will come to a gruesome pause:

And when they shall have finished their testimony, the beast that ascendeth out of the bottomless pit shall make war against them, and shall overcome them, and kill them. And their dead bodies shall lie in the street of the great city, which spiritually is called Sodom and Egypt, where also our Lord was crucified. And they of the people and kindreds and tongues and nations shall see their dead bodies three days and an half, and shall not suffer their dead bodies to be put into graves.
(REVELATION 11:7–9)

In other words, when the two witnesses finish their testimony, the protective hand of God will be lifted temporarily, so as to fulfill Scripture. They will be murdered by the antichrist and lie in the streets of Jerusalem for three and one-half days. Their bodies will be seen by the entire world, a concept that must have been unfathomable to John but makes perfect sense today with the advent of television and satellites. Observers will not bury them, perhaps because they will be afraid to do so, or maybe to establish this tragedy as a witness to the world or perhaps to prove that these men really are dead.

But an awesome thing is about to occur!

"And after three days and an half the Spirit of life from God entered into them, and they stood upon their feet; and great fear fell upon them which saw them. And they heard a great voice from heaven saying unto them, Come up hither. And they ascended up to heaven in a cloud; and their enemies beheld them" (Revelation 11:11–12).

Who are these two men? We don't know. The Bible doesn't come right out and tell us. But a fascinating code beginning in Zechariah 4:11–14 gives us some insight. The verse in which the code begins says this:

"Then answered I, and said unto him,What are these two olive trees upon the right side of the candlestick and upon the left side thereof? . . . Then said he, These are the two anointed ones, that stand by the Lord of the whole earth."

Who are the two olive trees, the two anointed ones? We can only speculate. But it is fascinating to note that within this very verse are encoded two names, each at an ELS of 36. The two names are "Elijah" and "Moses"!

The Mark that Protects the 144,000

During the early months of Tribulation, while the antichrist positions himself for international rule, the Holy Spirit will move upon the Earth within the hearts of men and women, turning them toward Christ. The Bible tells us that many people will accept Christ during this time.

Even at the midnight hour of God's wrath, we see a God who offers deliverance to whoever will call on His name!

Among those who accept Christ as their savior will be 144,000 from the nation of Israel. These 144,000 from across the globe will recognize that they are living in what the Scripture describes as the

Great Tribulation. They will also recognize that Christ is the true Messiah Who is judging the world. This 144,000 who accept Christ during the early months of the Tribulation will passionately promote the Gospel message.

Here are some of the insights the Bible gives us into these 144,000 Jewish believers:

Revelation 14:4 tells us that these individuals will be "redeemed from among men, being the firstfruits unto God and to the Lamb." This means that the 144,000 will walk in uprightness before God and will have accepted the Lamb of God (Jesus) as their Messiah. They will become the first people to receive Jesus during the Tribulation. Their witness will result in others being saved, including many Gentiles. Furthermore, these 144,000 will not only be saved, but they will be "sealed" in some fashion for their protection during the worst of the tribulation!

John writes:

And after these things I saw four angels standing on the four corners of the earth, holding the four winds of the earth, that the wind should not blow on the earth, nor on the sea, nor on any tree. And I saw another angel ascending from the east, having the seal of the living God: and he cried with a loud voice to the four angels, to whom it was given to hurt the earth and the sea, Saying, Hurt not the earth, neither the sea, nor the trees, till we have sealed the servants of our God in their foreheads. And I heard the number of them which were sealed: and there were sealed a hundred and forty and four thousand of all the tribes of the children of Israel.

(REVELATION 7:1–4)

Many have wondered about the exact nature of the mark that God will put on the 144,000 during the Tribulation period. Bible codes may give us some insights.

There is a verse in Ezekiel which refers to this same mark we find discussed in Revelation. Here's what the verse, found in Ezekiel 9:6, has to say: "Slay utterly old and young, both maids, and little children, and women: but come not near any man upon whom is the mark; and begin at my sanctuary. Then they began at the ancient men which were before the house [temple]."

Many encoded messages are found beginning within this verse that appear to give insights into the nature of this mark. For example, encoded from this verse at the ELS of -29 are the names "Jehovah" and "Jesus." Adjacent letters at the same ELS spell "the appointed seal for protection."

Now go with me to Exodus 19:14. Start with the fourth letter in the sixth word, then count in reverse every ninety-seventh letter and you will find the phrase "a vision of the mark of God," while adjacent letters at the same ELS spell "the exalted Father." In addition, the names of "Yeshua" and "Messiah" are located within encoded clusters around the above codes. Will the mark be the name of God? Time will tell. But isn't it interesting that Satan, the great counterfeiter, will put a mark representing the name of his evil representative on the hands or foreheads of those who would follow him?

Two other messages have been discovered originating from Ezekiel 9:6. The phrase "shall be his tattoo" has been discovered at an ELS of 36, while at an ELS of 46 we have found the phrase "the mark of the end time."

As a result of this mark, it appears that these 144,000 Jewish believers will be protected from God's wrath as well as from the wrath of the antichrist.

When it comes to the wrath of the antichrist, many Tribulation Saints will not be so lucky.

We have already seen, in Revelation 6:9–11, the poignant image of the souls of martyred Christians gathered under the throne of God, crying out in loud voices for God to avenge their deaths. John says that these men and women were "slain for the word of God, and for the testimony which they held." These slain believers are soothed with white robes and the instruction to "rest" until they are joined by the souls of additional men and women who, like them, will be martyred for their faith.

Now, in the final verses of chapter seven, we see the full impact of the events that were foretold: In Revelation 7:9–10, John describes a multitude standing before the throne, dressed in white and waving palm branches. Who are these souls? One of the elders explains to John:

> These are they which came out of great tribulation, and have washed their robes and made them white in the blood of the Lamb. Therefore are they before the throne of God, and serve him day and night in his temple: and he that sitteth on the throne shall dwell among them. They shall hunger no more, neither thirst any more; neither shall the sun light on them, nor any heat. For the Lamb which is in the midst of the throne shall feed them, and shall lead them unto living fountains of waters: and God shall wipe away all tears from their eyes.
>
> (REVELATION 7:14–17)

What a beautiful portrait of the heart of God as He cares tenderly for those who have suffered for his sake, providing them with His presence, shelter, food, water and comfort.

In fact, the depth of God's love for His own is perhaps illustrated by the fact that, immediately after wiping the tears of those who have suffered, God allows the opening of the seventh seal, unleashing the greatest display of His wrath the world has ever known. Indeed, the seventh seal contains the most catastrophic judgments imaginable! But before these judgments are allowed to unfold, John records a fascinating interlude in which God responds to the unanswered prayers of the Tribulation Saints.

Ah, but I'm getting ahead of the story. Let's take a look at all these events and more in Chapter 9!

NINE

When All Hell
Breaks Loose

B race yourself!

    If you thought the first six seals represented "hell on earth," you haven't seen anything yet. In fact, as Jesus opens the seventh seal, all of Heaven stands in silent awe of the horrors that will be rained down upon the earth.

As John observed, "And when he had opened the seventh seal, there was silence in heaven about the space of half an hour" (Revelation 8:1).

What a sobering image this is, as all of Heaven falls silent as God prepares to exact his final fury on the rebellious inhabitants of earth. Christ has opened the seventh seal and, as a result, a sequence of supernatural disasters are about to be unleashed on earth, the magnitude of which have never been experienced on our planet.

After thirty minutes of silence, Heaven prepares to mete out the judgments. John explains, "And I saw the seven angels which stood before God, and to them were given seven trumpets" (Revelation 8:2).

Seven trumpets, and each time a trumpet sounds earth will reel under the blow of wrath that will follow. The angels stand by, ready to sound the trumpets which will herald what are known as the seven "trumpet judgments."

But before these judgments begin, there is a brief interlude in which a very amazing scene takes place at the throne of God:

> *And another angel came and stood at the altar, having a golden censer; and there was given unto him much incense; that he should offer it with the prayers of all saints upon the golden altar which was before the throne. And the smoke of the incense which came with the prayers of the saints, ascended up before God out of the angel's hand. And the angel took the censer, and filled it with fire of the altar, and cast it into the earth: and there were voices, and thunderings, and lightnings, and an earthquake.*
>
> (REVELATION 8:2—5)

Consider this verse in light of Revelation 6:9–11, where martyred souls are told to rest awhile longer under the throne of God, and Revelation 7:17, where God wipes the tears from the eyes of those who have suffered. Now we see God respond to the precious incense of unanswered prayers.

These prayers undoubtedly represent many prayers for deliverance uttered by martyrs who have been waiting—some of them for centuries—for God to respond. And respond he does, with a display of shattering power! God is furious with the world for perse-cuting and martyring His believers. God responds with fire from his altar, triggering storms and an earthquake as a precursor to what will come as He continues to rain down his wrath on the na-tions that have cursed God and those He loves.

I would imagine that earth has yet to recover from the storms and earthquake they have just experienced when John sees Heaven gear up for the next round of catastrophes. Indeed, as he watches, "the seven angels which had the seven trumpets" prepare them-selves to sound.

The First Four of Seven Trumpet Judgments

The first angel sounded, and there followed hail and fire min-gled with blood, and they were cast upon the earth; and the third part of trees was burnt up, and all green grass was burnt up" (Revelation 8:7).

As this first trumpet sounds, one-third of the earth's surface goes up in smoke. This judgment is not unlike the judgment vis-ited on Sodom and Gomorrah, when God rained down burning sulfur. But Sodom and Gomorrah experienced God's wrath poured out on a small scale compared to what befalls earth here at God's ultimate wrath. With one-third of trees and grasses burned to the ground, the balance and ecology of the planet will be threatened. Undoubtedly, weather patterns will change dramatically due to the absence of vegetation, and major flooding and erosion will ensue.

As if this weren't enough, the following angels continue to blow their trumpets—heralding further catastrophes—in rapid-fire succession.

"And the second angel sounded, and as it were a great mountain burning with fire was cast into the sea: and the third part of the sea became blood; And the third part of the creatures which were in the sea, and had life, died; and the third part of the ships were destroyed" (Revelation 8:8–9).

Some scholars speculate that this event will be caused by a burning meteorite or asteroid crashing into the Mediterranean Sea, killing one third of sea life, destroying one third of the ships and turning the water to blood. In fact, the book of Daniel contains several encoded references to meteorites. The first occurs in the twelfth chapter of Daniel where we have discovered the Hebrew word for meteorite at an ELS of -97, while another, very stunning reference has been discovered in Daniel 4:32: "Alas! The prophesied meteor of greatness!" (first letter, first word, ELS of -198).

Scripture records another instance when God turned water into blood. The Nation of Israel had served as Egypt's slaves for many years when God sent Moses to the Pharaoh with the message that he was to let God's people go. When the Pharaoh refused, God punished Egypt with ten different plagues—one of these plagues consisting of all the water in Egypt being turned into blood. Here's what happened:

And the Lord spake unto Moses, Say unto Aaron, Take thy rod, and stretch out thine hand upon the waters of Egypt, upon their streams,

upon their rivers, and upon their ponds, and upon all their pools of wa-
ter, that they may become blood; and that there may be blood through-
out all the land of Egypt, both in vessels of wood, and in vessels of stone.
(EXODUS 7:19)

How the people suffered as every lake, pond and river—even drinking water stored in clay pots—was transformed into blood.

The plagues on Egypt appear to foreshadow the final judgments that God will enact on all the nations of the earth. In fact, three of the Egyptian plagues—water turned to blood, painful boils and darkness—are very similar to three of the trumpet judgments. Furthermore, I believe that the transformation of the water into blood is nothing less than a metaphor of the bloody battle of Armageddon that will soon take place. In fact, encoded in Exodus 7:19, starting with the first letter in the eighteenth word, counting forward every seventh letter is the phrase "shall be the valley of blood," which alludes to the culmination of the seventh trumpet judgment—the bloody battle of Armageddon—which will take place in the Valley of Megiddo.

Following the second trumpet judgment, John continues his description of the remaining five judgments:

And the third angel sounded, and there fell a great star from
heaven, . . . and it fell upon the third part of the rivers, and upon the
fountains of waters; And the name of the star is called Wormwood: and
the third part of the waters became wormwood; and many men died of
the waters, because they were made bitter.
(REVELATION 8:10–11)

Scholars speculate that an asteroid named Wormwood will strike the earth with such force that it buries itself deep in the ground and pollutes a major water source. A Bible code in Ezekiel 22 actually contains the word "wormwood" at an ELS of 59.

"And the fourth angel sounded, and the third part of the sun was smitten, and the third part of the moon, and the third part of the stars; so as the third part of them was darkened, and the day shone not for a third part of it, and the night likewise" (Revelation 8:12).

The fourth judgment affects the sun, moon, and stars—heavenly bodies earth depends upon—turning one-third of them dark. Some speculate that this event will reverse the day-to-night ratio— sixteen hours of darkness to eight hours of light each day.

This effect could result from a massive volcanic eruption. Geologists say that Yellowstone Park is, in fact, the result of a huge volcano that erupted thousands of years ago, killing all life within a thousand miles and covering the terrain with lava. Volcanic eruptions this large can change weather patterns and spew ash and dust into the atmosphere, darkening the sun, moon, and stars.

In fact, ancient writings from A.D. 535 tell of a darkening of the sun that lasted eighteen months and a global cooling trend that lasted a full decade. Crops failed as famine and starvation threat- ened the globe. Scientists speculate that this condition could have been caused by either a comet or an asteroid entering the earth's atmosphere and exploding, or perhaps by a catastrophic volcanic eruption, kicking up dust and debris that hung in the atmosphere around earth, thereby darkening the sun. Indeed, volcanic erup- tions located near the equator can throw enough dust and debris into the atmosphere to cover both hemispheres of earth.

What other kind of impact can a volcanic eruption have on planet earth?

Writings from February A.D. 535 describe a deafening explosion heard in China from a volcanic eruption. Other writings housed in the Royal Palace in Java, known as "The Book of Kings," tell of a mighty thunder accompanied by torrential rain and hail and a darkening of the sky. The aftermath of this mighty thunder was called an "eternal winter."

Most of us in affluent countries cannot even imagine what it would be like to experience a cataclysmic event of this proportion. But we have writings from 1883 that describe the volcanic eruption of Krakatoa on the islands of Indonesia. These writings describe not only the horrors of hot lava and ash, but also the impact of colossal tidal waves that swept unknown numbers of people out to sea. In fact, for months after the eruption, the Sunda Straits were congested with thick banks of cooled lava—called pumice—which contained the corpses of many who had drowned. Two weeks after the disaster, one observer wrote:

> *Thousands of corpses of human beings and also carcasses of animals still await burial, and make their presence apparent by the indescribable stench. They lie in knots and entangled masses impossible to unravel, and often jammed along with coconut stems among all that had served these thousands as dwellings, furniture, farming implements, and adornments for houses and compounds.*

Almost forty miles away, on the island of Sumatra, a woman described her experience on the morning that the aftermath of the volcanic eruption and ensuing tidal wave hit her village, killing some and sparing others.

Suddenly, it became pitch dark. The last thing I saw was the ash being pushed up through the cracks in the floorboards, like a fountain. I turned to my husband and heard him say in despair 'Where is the knife?' . . . I will cut all our wrists and then we shall be released from our suffering sooner.' The knife could not be found. I felt a heavy pressure, throwing me to the ground. Then it seemed as if all the air was being sucked away and I could not breathe. . . . I felt people rolling over me. . . . No sound came from my husband or children. . . . I remember thinking, I want to . . . go outside . . . but I could not straighten my back. . . . I tottered, doubled up, to the door. . . . I forced myself through the opening. . . . I tripped and fell. I realized the ash was hot and I tried to protect my face with my hands. The hot bite of the pumice pricked like needles. . . . Without thinking, I walked hopefully forward. Had I been in my right mind, I would have understood what a dangerous thing it was to . . . plunge into the hellish darkness. . . . I ran up against . . . branches and did not even think of avoiding them. I entangled myself more and more. . . . My hair got caught up. . . . I noticed for the first time that [my] skin was hanging off everywhere, thick and moist from the ash stuck to it. Thinking it must be dirty, I wanted to pull bits of skin off, but that was still more painful. . . . I did not know I had been burnt.

Magnify these vivid and terrifying images many times, and perhaps you will catch a glimpse of the kind of suffering that will be experienced during the outpouring of God's wrath.

In fact, a prophetic passage in the book of Isaiah gives us these terrifying images from the future:

Howl ye; for the day of the Lord is at hand; it shall come as a destruction from the Almighty. Therefore shall all hands be faint, and every man's heart shall melt: And they shall be afraid: pangs and sorrows shall take hold of them; they shall be in pain as a woman that travaileth: they shall be amazed one at another; their faces shall be as flames. Behold, the day of the Lord cometh, cruel both with wrath and fierce anger, to lay the land desolate: and he shall destroy the sinners thereof out of it. For the stars of heaven and the constellations thereof shall not give their light: the sun shall be darkened in his going forth, and the moon shall not cause her light to shine. And I will punish the world for their iniquity; and I will cause the arrogancy of the proud to cease, and will lay low the haughtiness of the terrible. . . . Therefore I will shake the heavens, and the earth shall remove out of her place, in the wrath of the Lord of hosts, and in the day of his fierce anger. . . . they shall every man turn to his own people, and flee every one into his own land. Every one that is found shall be thrust through; and every one that is joined unto them shall fall by the sword. Their children shall also be dashed to pieces before their eyes; their houses shall be spoiled, and their wives ravished.

(ISAIAH 13:6—16)

"Woe, Woe, Woe to the Inhabiters of the Earth!"

The first four trumpets of judgment have sounded and horrendous disaster has befallen the Earth. God's wrath has all but destroyed the planet! One third of all vegetation has burned up, major water sources have been poisoned, the sun, moon and stars are dimmed by one third. Mother Earth groans under the heavy hand of God's rage.

Yet three more judgments await, and—as hard as it is to believe—these three are the worst of the lot. Perhaps what is even more mind-boggling is the fact that, in the midst of these terrors, the arrogant and rebellious nations still refuse to repent or even acknowledge their need for God!

At this point, John sees an angel fly across Heaven and shout, "Woe, woe, woe to the inhabiters of the earth by reason of the other voices of the trumpet of the three angels, which are yet to sound!" Based on this verse, the next three trumpet judgments are also referred to as the first, second and third woes.

And the fifth angel sounded, and I saw a star fall from heaven unto the earth: and to him was given the key of the bottomless pit. And he opened the pit, and there arose a smoke out of the pit, as the smoke of a great furnace; and the sun and the air were darkened by reason of the smoke of the pit. And there came out of the smoke locusts upon the earth: and unto them was given power, as the scorpions of the earth have power. And it was commanded them that they should not hurt the grass of the

earth, neither any green thing, neither any tree; but only those men that have not the seal of God in their foreheads. And to them it was given that they should not kill them, but that they should be tormented five months: and their torment was as the torment of a scorpion, when he striketh a man. And in those days shall men seek death, and shall not find it; and shall desire to die, and death will flee from them.
(REVELATION 9:1–6)

Scripture goes on to describe these locusts in great detail. They appear like horses with faces like men, wearing gold crowns on their heads with teeth like lions and hair like women. They wear breastplates and their wings sound like many horses and chariots running to battle. These tails look like serpents with heads. Out of their mouths issue fire, smoke and brimstone. They number two hundred thousand thousand, representing a number that cannot be calculated, and the king of these locusts is an evil demon from the bottomless pit named Abaddon in Hebrew and Apollyon in Greek, meaning destroyer.

These creatures sting like scorpions. The sting of a scorpion is very painful, sending venom into the veins, seeming to set the body on fire. The scorpion sting seldom kills, but makes one extremely sick for five days. The Bible says that the sickness from *these* stings will hurt for five *months* and cause such misery that people will cry out to die, but death will not come to relieve their suffering.

Yet even this terrible woe will be eclipsed by the next judgment, which is far more severe, inflicting not only pain but death on those who do not bear the seal of God.

When the sixth angel sounds the trumpet, a voice shouts, "Loose the four angels which are bound in the great river Euphrates." These four evil demons have been bound by God until this time and are now loosed to sweep across earth, killing one third of humanity—estimated at about one and a half billion people.

At this point, God's righteous anger has pummeled earth with disaster after disaster. The oceans and waves roar from severe storm patterns created by the dimming of the sun, moon and stars. Tidal waves pound shorelines, earthquakes devastate areas that have never before experienced earthquakes, killing thousands of people. One third of all trees on earth have burned. The balance of the seasons and weather patterns has shifted. There are probably only eight hours of light per day. Earth's resources are contaminated, her ecosystems completely destroyed. Millions have died.

And there is no way to escape! Even as men manage to evade one catastrophe, they will fall victim to the next or the next! Indeed, as the prophet Isaiah foresaw:

> *The land shall be utterly emptied, and utterly spoiled: for the Lord hath spoken this word. The earth mourneth and fadeth away, the haughty people of the earth do languish. The earth also is defiled under the inhabitants thereof; because they have transgressed the laws, changed the ordinance, broken the everlasting covenant. Therefore hath the curse devoured the earth, and they that dwell therein are desolate: therefore the inhabitants of the earth are burned, and few men left. . . .*
>
> *Fear, and the pit, and the snare, are upon thee, O inhabitant of the earth. And it shall come to pass, that he who fleeth from the noise of*

the fear shall fall into the pit; and he that cometh up out of the midst of the pit shall be taken in the snare: for the windows from on high are open, and the foundations of the earth do shake. The earth is utterly broken down, the earth is clean dissolved, the earth is moved exceedingly.

(ISAIAH 24:3–6, 17–19)

And *still* the Bible tells us that "the rest of the men which were not killed by these plagues yet repented not," but continued with their evil works which included devil worship, the crafting and worship of idols, theft, murders, fornication and sorcery (Revelation 9:20–21).

The Seventh Trumpet Sounds and the Seven Bowl Judgments Begin

Perhaps you are thinking, "Things can't possibly get any worse! Thank God, there is only one trumpet left to go!"

This is true. But—not unlike a Russian nesting doll that, once opened, reveals more dolls inside—the blast of the seventh trumpet (also known as the third woe) introduces not just *one* but *seven* more judgments!

The seven judgments that are introduced by the blast of the seventh trumpet are contained in vials and delivered by seven angels. Because these judgments are pictured as being "poured out" onto the earth, they are known as the seven bowl judgments, and as you might guess, conditions on earth continue to spiral as these judgments are fulfilled.

Here is John's description of the scene in Heaven where seven angels are tasked with the deliverance of these last and most terrible judgments:

> And after that I looked, and, behold, the temple of the tabernacle of the testimony in heaven was opened: And the seven angels came out of the temple, having the seven plagues, clothed in pure and white linen, and having their breasts girded with golden girdles. And one of the four [living creatures] gave unto the seven angels seven golden vials full of the wrath of God, who liveth for ever and ever. And the temple was filled with smoke from the glory of God, and from his power; and no man was able to enter into the temple, till the seven plagues of the seven angels were fulfilled. And I heard a great voice out of the temple saying to the seven angels, Go your ways, and pour out the vials of the wrath of God upon the earth.
>
> (REVELATION 15:5—8, 16:1)

Reading these words, I am struck by the solemnity of what is occurring. These seven angels appear to receive their commission in the Holy Temple in Heaven. Clothed and girded for their task, they exit the Temple, accept the vials of wrath and are dispatched by the voice of God himself.

Without further ado, the first angel fulfills his duty. John writes: "And the first went, and poured out his vial upon the earth; and there fell a noisome and grievous sore upon the men which had the mark of the beast, and upon them which worshipped his image" (Revelation 16:2).

This first bowl judgment is often referred to as the "plague of boils." The Living Bible calls these boils "horrible, malignant sores" and, indeed, the word "boils" has been discovered encoded in many prophetic passages. According to the Revelation, this plague is intended for only those who bear the mark of the beast and worship the antichrist. Just as God protected His people from the Egyptian plagues, it appears that in the final hours he again protects his own—the 144,000 as well as the Tribulation Saints who have refused to worship the antichrist.

"And the second angel poured out his vial upon the sea; and it became as the blood of a dead man: and every living soul died in the sea. And the third angel poured out his vial upon the rivers and fountains for waters; and they became blood."

As the second and third angels pour out their vials, all of the oceans and waterways of the earth are either turned to blood or become as blood. You may recall that the second trumpet judgment turned one third of the seas to blood, but here at the second and third bowl judgments, God turns *all* of the water on the earth to blood and everything in them dies.

Why blood?

One of the angels gives the answer: "Thou art righteous, O Lord, which art, and wast, and shalt be, because thou has judged thus. For they [the unrighteous on earth] have shed the blood of saints and prophets, and thou hast given them blood to drink, for they are worthy [to be punished in this manner]."

Are these waters turned into actual blood? Some scholars say yes. Others say no, focusing on the part of Scripture that says the waters will become "*as* the blood of a dead man"—congealing and contaminated. Regardless of the interpretation, the significance

of these verses is clear. Whether the seas and rivers are blood or
like blood, earth's ecology will be irreparable.

Two thirds of the earth is water. One of the key essentials of life will
no longer be available. Water supplies will become disease-ridden.
Imagine the stench of rotting sea life, not to mention the toll this
judgment will exact on the fishing industry, commercial shipping
and international military naval fleets. In addition, this plague will
probably severely disable or even halt the world's ability to gener-
ate electricity, since most power plants are driven by water or steam.

To make matters worse, as the fourth bowl judgment is spilled
onto the earth, the result is an unprecedented heat wave that
scorches the inhabitants of earth. And there will be no pure water
to cool or quench this heat.

Do the people of earth now recognize the error of their ways?
Do they fall to their knees and plead with God for mercy? Do they
ask God to forgive their evil acts? Not on your life! Scripture tells
us that, instead, they curse the name of God.

The Old Testament prophet Malachi foreshadowed this judgment when he prophesied:

> *For, behold, the day cometh, that shall burn as an oven; and all the*
> *proud, yea, and all that do wickedly, shall be stubble: and the day that*
> *cometh shall burn them up, saith the Lord of hosts, that it shall leave*
> *them neither root nor branch. But unto you that fear my name shall the*
> *Sun of righteousness arise with healing in his wings; and ye shall go*
> *forth, and grow up as calves of the stall.*
>
> (MALACHI 4:1–2)

Notice how, even at the midnight hour, God offers healing to those who will turn to Him and honor His name. Indeed, God's mercy is long-suffering! Though many still curse Him, the good news is that in the midst of the bloodcurdling horrors of the final hours, many will repent, wailing, "Mother was right!" or "The preacher was right! I should have listened! Oh, why was I such a fool!" At this point, the decision to follow Jesus may well mean a martyr's death. But for those who give up their lives to follow Christ, there will be healing and prosperity and safety in heaven!

Unfortunately, for the unrepentant heart, there is no mercy.

The fifth bowl judgment focuses on the headquarters of the antichrist. Some scriptures refer to the antichrist's headquarters as Babylon, but I believe that this is a metaphor for the actual city of Rome, which will serve as the antichrist's center for religion, government, and commerce. Here's what John saw: "And the fifth angel poured out his vial upon the seat of the beast; and his kingdom was full of darkness; and they gnawed their tongues for pain, And blasphemed the God of heaven because of their pains and their sores, and repented not of their deeds" (Revelation 16:10–11).

The Bible doesn't indicate how long this darkness will last, but some scholars believe it will be exacerbated due to fact that power plants have shut down, unable to function because the waters of the world no longer flow, but are instead thick and congealing.

The Final Bowl Judgments
and the Road to Armageddon

And the sixth angel poured out his vial upon the great river Euphrates;
and the water thereof was dried up, that the way of the kings of the east
might be prepared. And I saw three unclean spirits like frogs come out of
the mouth of the dragon, and out of the mouth of the beast, and out
of the mouth of the false prophet. For they are the spirits of devils, work-
ing miracles, which go forth unto the kings of the earth and of the whole
world, to gather them to the battle of that great day of God Almighty.
(REVELATION 16:12—14)

Bible codes have been discovered in Daniel—in surface text that
vividly describes the antichrist—that appear to refer to this sixth
bowl judgment. Go to the second letter of the third word of Daniel
11:36 and you will find, at an ELS of 128, the phrase "from the evil
demon." Daniel 11:37 (third letter, eighth word, ELS of -30) contains the encryption "possessed with a demon" while adjacent letters contain the encrypted words "Euphrates River."

This judgment not only reveals the nature of three of the
demons possessing the antichrist and false prophet, it also dries
up the Euphrates River—or whatever thick, clotting mess the river
has turned into—which creates a dry path where there had once
been a formidable barrier.

Since the beginning of time, the Euphrates River has created a
natural border between east and west. With that barrier removed,

the "kings of the east"—armed forces from the Orient—will be free to travel west. Some scholars believe these armies will travel west in order to engage and defeat the armies of the antichrist. Many Bible scholars believe that these eastern armies, duped and incited by evil demons, will travel west in order to join the antichrist in an attack on Jerusalem.

Indeed, these eastern armies have plenty of company, because three evil spirits—John says they are "like frogs"—have been busy circulating among the kings and leaders of the world, stirring them up.

I believe that the kings and leaders of the world will be incited to look upon Israel, the Jews and the God who loves them as the reason for the chaos, death and destruction that has engulfed the planet. Deceived by Satan, these leaders may well come to the conclusion that the way to put an end to the suffering is to converge on Jerusalem and level the Holy City once and for all.

But this is more than a showdown between nations. The real showdown is between one demonic egomaniac and the Almighty Creator and King. Indeed, this is Satan's last ditch effort to wage war against God Himself. It is a futile effort, of course, but that doesn't diminish the waste and carnage that comes from the resulting bloodbath.

Even in Bible codes we see images of preparations for great battle. The following codes have all been found in the twelfth chapter of Daniel which, as we have already discovered, is devoted to the end times both in surface text as well as literally hundreds of encoded messages:

"His great missile" (12:1, fourth letter, twenty-fourth word, ELS of 22)

"tanks" (12:8, first letter, seventh word, ELS of 17)

"for their war" (12:10, third letter, eleventh word, ELS of 19)

"strong, afflicting armor" (12:5, first letter, eleventh word, ELS of -66)

"the rain of missiles" (12:10, third letter, first word, ELS of -176)

"the enemy satellite of death" (12:5, third letter, thirteenth word, ELS of -47)

"the gun (rifle)" (12:3, second letter, fourth word, ELS of -50)

"gunfire" (12:6, fifth letter, seventh word, ELS of -30)

"knowledge of military intelligence" (12:5, third letter, eighth word, ELS of -7)

"military invasion" (12:7, second letter, twenty-third word, ELS of -137)

"the remarkable destruction of the Bear" (12:7, second letter, twenty-third word, ELS of -22)

"the great mystery Babylon" (5:3, first letter, tenth word, ELS of 32)

What we know for sure is that all of the kings and leaders of the world will amass their armies and head toward the Valley of Megiddo—which today is known as the Valley of Jezreel—about fifty miles north from Jerusalem.

How many troops might this entail?

It was estimated in 1980 that all the nations of the world could muster a combined total of approximately five hundred million armed troops. Today, that figure has risen to at least six or seven hundred million. Even taking into consideration the many draft-eligible men who will have already died from starvation, plagues and other reasons, the number of battle-ready men who will converge at the Valley of Megiddo will be epic.

Can you imagine the logistics of moving armies comprising multiplied millions? Some of the nations involved with this diabolical crusade will be on the opposite side of the globe, but God will prepare the way for them to keep their appointment with destiny. Picture, for a moment, an army of two hundred million from the east, forging their way through out-of-control weather conditions, pushing ever forward to their predestined place in history.

As you can imagine, these troops will experience health problems on a scale never before imagined, due to the many plagues and polluted air and water sources. Water, as we've seen, has become unusable, and the air as well may be toxic as a result of the worldwide deployment of biological and atomic weapons.

To make matters worse, as these armies are gathering, the Lord lets loose with the seventh bowl judgment. As soon as the last vial is emptied, God himself proclaims that—with this seventh bowl judgment, this third woe, this seventh judgment of the seventh seal—the Tribulation is finished. Then the judgment is delivered, this time in the form of storms, lethal hail and an earthquake so massive that mountains are leveled and the antichrist's headquarters split into three.

Here is what John observes:

And the seventh angel poured out his vial into the air; and there came a great voice out of the temple of heaven, from the throne, saying, It is done. And there were voices, and thunders, and lightnings; and there was a great earthquake, such as was not since men were upon the earth, so mighty an earthquake, and so great. And the great city was divided into three parts, and the cities of the nations fell: and great Babylon came in remembrance before God, to give unto her the cup of the wine of the fierceness of his wrath. And every island fled away, and the mountains were not found. And there fell upon men a great hail out of heaven, every stone about the weight of a talent: and men blasphemed God because of the plague of the hail; for the plague thereof was exceeding great.

(REVELATION 16:17—21)

"Every stone about the weight of a talent"? What exactly does that mean?

These hailstones will weigh between sixty and 130 pounds.

To my knowledge, one atmospheric aberration has come close to the event described in Revelation. During atomic bomb testing on Bikini Island in 1946, the island was pummeled by hail weighing up to one hundred pounds. Apparently, the atomic reaction in the atmosphere had created a mutation that caused an imbalance in the atomic structure of the elements.

This catastrophic event will be repeated during the seventh plague. In fact, it's entirely possible that God will use the activity of advanced nuclear weapons unleashed by war-hungry nations to create the phenomenon of 130-pound hailstones. Whatever the cause, the Bible is clear about what will happen. In fact, encoded in

Daniel 12:6 (second letter, third word, ELS of -11) is encoded the phrase "hail shall afflict." In Psalm 10:1–2, where the surface text reads, "Why standest thou afar off, O Lord? Why hidest thou thy self in time of trouble? The wicked in his pride doth persecute the poor: let them be taken in the devices that they have imagined," we have discovered encrypted the phrase "the plagues for the evil" as well as the words "hail" and "talent," referring to the weight of the stones.

In Ezekiel 22:31, where the surface text quotes the Lord as saying, "Therefore have I poured out mine indignation upon them; I have consumed them with the fire of my wrath: their own way have I recompensed upon their heads," we have found yet another reference to "hail." How interesting that, when it comes to compensating the wicked for their sins, the Lord promises to heap their payment upon their heads—and then sends judgment in the form of killer hailstones falling from the sky.

Even *average*-sized hailstones have resulted in the death of humans. On April 30, 1888, in northern India, 246 people were killed, some by suffocation under mounds of hail, many by being struck directly by half-pound hailstones. In the Sichuan Province of China in 1986, more than a hundred people were killed in a hailstorm where the largest stones weighed two pounds. Imagine the toll in human life that will be exacted by hailstones weighing not half a pound or two pounds but up to *one hundred and thirty pounds*! In fact, many scholars believe that a portion of the military forces approaching the Valley of Megiddo will be destroyed by this hailstorm.

And yet, despite lethal hail, boils, earthquakes, thirst, the leveling of familiar landmarks and the challenges of traveling through terrain upended by destruction, these armies will be unstoppable. The Bible tells us that these armies will converge on the Valley of Megiddo in Northern Israel from all parts of the globe—north, south, east and west. Imagine all the armies of the world led by high-ranking generals who will, upon arrival, relinquish their authority to the antichrist and false prophet for final engagement of war! Imagine six hundred million troops, prepared to do the bidding of the antichrist as he orchestrates what he believes will be the final blow against a Holy God and the people He loves!

Who will fight for Jerusalem?

Certainly a remnant of the nation of Israel will fight for Jerusalem.

Many Jews who, up to this point, have escaped annihilation will return to Israel and reoccupy their beloved city. We know there will be surviving Jews because of the following prophetic Scripture recorded in Zechariah 13:8–9:

> And it shall come to pass, that in all the land, saith the Lord, two parts therein shall be cut off and die; but the third shall be left therein. And I will bring the third part through the fire, and will refine them as silver is refined, and will try them as gold is tried: they shall call on my name, and I will hear them: I will say, It is my people: and they shall say, The Lord is my God.

It is estimated that there are about 18 million Jews in the world today who do not believe that Jesus is the Messiah. If the Tribulation were to begin in the very near future, this is how many Jews would have to face the Tribulation. If two thirds of these 18 million who reject Christ are cut off and experience physical and spiritual death, that leaves approximately six million in the nation of Israel who will be refined—as silver and gold is refined—through the fire of suffering, who will call on the name of the Lord, of whom God will say, "It is my people," and who will respond by saying, "The Lord is my God!"

I can imagine that a portion of these will be present in the city of Jerusalem to defend the city. And yet, even an army of six million would fall quickly against an opposing force of six *hundred* million.

Again I ask, *who will fight for Jerusalem?*

TEN

The Day of the Lord

And I saw heaven opened, and behold a white horse; and he that sat upon him was called Faithful and True, and in righteousness he doth judge and make war. His eyes were as a flame of fire, and on his head were many crowns; and he had a name written, that no man knew, but he himself. And he was clothed with a vesture dipped in blood: and his name is called The Word of God. And the armies which were in heaven followed him upon white horses, clothed in fine linen, white and clean.

And out of his mouth goeth a sharp sword, that with it he should smite the nations: and he shall rule them with a rod of iron: and he treadeth the winepress of the fierceness and wrath of Almighty God. And he hath on his vesture and on his thigh a name written, KING OF KINGS, AND LORD OF LORDS.

(REVELATION 19:11—16)

W ho will fight for Israel?
And for the raptured Church?
And for the martyred saints?
And for you and for me?

The Warrior has arrived. He is judge, jury, executioner and king all rolled into one. He has fire in his eyes and the power of life and death in his words. He has already drawn first blood, yet is accompanied by fresh armies. What he is about to do to his enemies is not unlike someone treading in a vat of ripe grapes, reducing them to empty skins and staining the ground red with their juices. He is called The Word of God, King of Kings and Lord of Lords.

He is Jesus Christ!

When Jesus returns to rescue Israel and punish the wicked by "treading the winepress of the wrath of God," there will actually be more than one battle to devastate Israel. This series of battles is known as Armageddon.

While the Bible doesn't give us all the specifics as to time and place, we know that the 180-mile-long Valley of Megiddo will play an important role as the armies of the world converge on this spot in order to prepare for battle. Many scholars believe that the Valley of Jehoshaphat (Joel 3:11–15), the Jordan Valley and Dead Sea (Joel 2:20; Revelation 14:20) as well as the mountains of Moab, Edom and Bozrah in modern Jordan (Isaiah 34:5–9; 63:1–6) will be battle sites as well. Finally, the city of Jerusalem will see much bloodshed as the city is captured, recaptured and captured again. Indeed, many Jews in Israel will be killed and half the city taken.

Listen to one prophet's description of the brutality unleashed when Jerusalem falls to the armies of the world: "Behold, the day of the Lord cometh, and thy spoil shall be divided in the midst of thee. For I will gather all nations against Jerusalem to battle; and the city shall be taken, and the houses rifled, and the women ravished; and half of the city shall go forth into captivity, and the residue of the people shall not be cut off from the city" (Zechariah 14:1–2).

But despite the loss of half of the city and many of those defending it, what we will soon see is that the vengeance of God will not go unsatisfied. In Zechariah 12:11 we find this phrase "In that day shall there be a great mourning in Jerusalem, as the mourning of Hadadrimmon in the valley of Mediggon." Encoded in this verse (first letter, seventh word, ELS of 3) is the phrase "mountain of his vengeance" that appears to describe the magnitude of wrath that will be exacted in these final battles! Another code that appears to refer to the crushing bloodbath of God's wrath is Daniel 12:12 (third letter, third word, ELS of 43), where we have discovered the encoded phrase "great winepress."

Indeed, the prophet Joel describes God's wrath not only as a winepress and the Great Supper of God, but also as a sickle, harvesting the wicked!

Let the heathen be wakened, and come up to the valley of Jehoshaphat: for there will I sit to judge all the heathen round about. Put ye in the sickle, for the harvest is ripe: come, get you down; for the press is full, the fats overflow; for their wickedness is great. Multitudes, multitudes in the valley of decision: for the day of the Lord is near in the valley of de-

cision. The sun and the moon shall be darkened, and the stars shall
withdraw their shining.

(JOEL 3:12–15)

According to this verse, just prior to the battles of Armageddon,
darkness will descend on the earth, causing confusion among the
troops gathered for battle. Many believe that the troops of the antichrist will respond with the deployment of weaponry and, in the
confusion, will kill many of their own in so-called "friendly fire."

And their woes are just beginning. Pay attention to the prophetic
images given to us through the prophet Zephaniah, images of wrath,
distress, desolation, darkness and death:

The great day of the Lord is near, it is near, and hasteth greatly, even
the voice of the day of the Lord: the mighty man shall cry there bitterly.
That day is a day of wrath, a day of trouble and distress, a day of waste-
ness and desolation, a day of darkness and gloominess, a day of clouds
and thick darkness, A day of the trumpet and alarm against the fenced
cities, and against the high towers. And I will bring distress upon men,
that they shall walk like blind men, because they have sinned against
the Lord: and their blood shall be poured out as dust, and their flesh as
the dung.

(ZEPHANIAH 1:14–17)

What a horrible description of the wrath of God that will be dis-
played at the battles of Armageddon. Brave men shall cry aloud.
Blood shall be poured out as dust, referring to the fact that men's
blood will be as valueless and pervasive as dust. They shall walk as

blind men. This statement gives the impression that the armies will be so duped and drugged by hatred that nothing will deter them from their goal of the annihilation of Israel and the righteous God of Heaven.

There is another verse as well which describes the mindless determination of the antichrist's armies: "Before their face the people shall be much pained: all faces shall gather blackness. They shall run like mighty men; they shall climb the wall like men of war; and they shall march every one on his ways, and they shall not break their ranks" (Joel 2:6–7).

Now let us return to Revelation's brutal account of the final hours, found in the fourteenth and nineteenth chapters of Revelation. John's description of how God not only wins the war, but disposes of the carnage of Armageddon, is chilling indeed:

And I saw an angel standing in the sun; and he cried with a loud voice, saying to all the fowls that fly in the midst of heaven, Come and gather yourselves together unto the supper of the great God; that ye may eat the flesh of kings, and the flesh of captains, and the flesh of mighty men, and the flesh of horses, and of them that sit on them, and the flesh of all men, both free and bond, both small and great. And I saw the beast, and the kings of the earth, and their armies, gathered together to make war against him that sat on the horse, and against his army. And the beast was taken, and with him the false prophet that wrought miracles before him, with which he had deceived them that had received the mark of the beast, and them that worshipped his image. These both were cast alive into a lake of fire burning with brimstone. And the remnant were slain with the sword of him that sat upon the horse, which sword proceeded out of his mouth: and all the fowls were filled with their flesh.

(REVELATION 19:17–21)

And I looked, and behold a white cloud, and upon the cloud one sat like unto the Son of man, having on his head a golden crown, and in his hand a sharp sickle. And another angel came out of the temple, crying with a loud voice to him that sat on the cloud, Thrust in thy sickle, and reap: for the time is come for thee to reap; for the harvest of the earth is ripe. And he that sat on the cloud thrust in his sickle on the earth; and the earth was reaped. And another angel came out of the temple which is in heaven, he also having a sharp sickle. And another angel came out from the altar, which had power over fire; and cried with a loud voice to him that had the sharp sickle, saying, Thrust in my sharp sickle, and gather the clusters of the vine of the earth; for her grapes are fully ripe. And the angel thrust in his sickle into the earth, and gathered the vine of the earth, and cast it into the great winepress of the wrath of God.

(REVELATION 14:14–19)

And the winepress was trodden without the city, and blood came out of the winepress, even unto the horse bridles, by the space of a thousand and six hundred furlongs. [The Living Bible computes this at 200 miles.]

(REVELATION 14:20)

Wow!

Blood flowing up to the bridle of a horse, and all the fowls of the air feasting on the flesh of the dead! Can there be any question that the wicked have paid the greatest possible price for their brutality and rebellion?

I know it's difficult to imagine the amount of blood that would have to be shed in order to flow as high as the bridle of a horse—approximately five feet! And yet remember that the Battles of Armageddon take place in valleys, not to mention the fact that these valleys—normally scorching and arid—have recently been pounded with one-hundred-pound hailstones! I believe that it is the mingling of the melting hailstones and rain with the spilled blood of slain armies that creates blood-red rivers—perhaps even flash floods—coursing through these valleys to the depth of five feet! Even Bible codes refer to this nightmarish event: In Exodus 7:19 at an ELS of 7 is encoded the phrase "shall be the valley of blood," while in Zechariah 12:10 (second letter, nineteenth word, ELS of -183) is the equally chilling phrase "the river of blood."

How these awesome events unfold remains to be seen. But one thing is certain beyond a shadow of doubt:

Jesus Christ—The Word of God, King of Kings and Lord of Lords—will rescue Israel, avenge those who have suffered in his name, punish the wicked, redeem the earth, imprison Satan, and reign victorious over the earth.

Should We Be Afraid?

When we began this journey together, we asked a series of crucial questions:

"Are we living in the end times?"

"Is life on earth as we know it drawing to a close?"

"Is Jesus really coming soon? And if he is, what difference should that make in my life?

And finally, "Should I be afraid?"

In some regards, I imagine that my answer to that last question will depend on how *you* have decided to respond to the choice that Jesus Christ extends to you with nail-scarred hands, saying, "I love you! Will you accept the gift of salvation and eternal life that I have secured for you with my death on the cross?"

If you respond to the choice by saying "no," then you may well live in fear, for in rejecting the gift of Life extended to you by a Holy God, you are casting your lot with those who have also rejected him, the same people who—as we have just seen—will pay for their decision with their blood and flesh and with their eternal souls.

However, if you respond to Jesus' offer with a resounding "Yes!" then you have nothing to fear, for you belong to the King and Victor who has not only your future but the future of our entire planet securely in the palm of his hand!

How securely does He hold the future, your personal future and the future of the world as well?

We have just seen how his ironclad grasp on the future allowed him to, thousands of years ago, craft a book that foretold the future in both its surface text and in thousands of hidden messages encrypted—like a crossword puzzle—within the text as well. Secular statisticians determine that the odds of these words and phrases occurring in the way that they do are 1 to the 100th power, which is the same as saying they are beyond random chance. In addition to being statistically impossible, these Bible codes have also given us insights into what God has planned. They have also given us hope as we grow in our understanding that there *is* a plan, that events yet to come are not random, coincidental or capricious, but instead are nothing less than the divine strategy of an all-knowing, all-powerful and all-righteous God who loves us with an everlasting love!

We are nearing the final pages of this book, but before we part company for now, I would like to present—as further proof of God's unerring hand on the future of our planet and your personal future as well—two final examples of hidden messages in the Bible. These messages, like the others we've examined, are irrefutable proof that there *is* a God, and that *He knows.* We have examined some amazing codes, you and I, but beyond anything that we've seen so far, these next two hidden messages create in me a sense of awe and worship, and I think they just might do the same for you.

"Why Do We Deal Treacherously One Man Against His Brother?"

Trinity Broadcasting recently aired a series of programs titled "Creation in the 21st Century," hosted by Carl Baugh. In putting together the program, Carl turned to the computer skills of research associate Dr. Larry Mitcham.

Let me tell you a few things about Larry. A retired engineer from Texas Instruments, Larry breathes, eats and sleeps computers. He understands computer systems forward, backward and inside out. When Carl asked Larry to write a program that would search the Bible for codes associated with the September 11 terrorist attack on the World Trade Center, Larry knew just what to do.

What he discovered still gives me goosebumps to this day:

Emanating from the text of a single verse—Psalm 23:4—Larry uncovered a tight cluster of hidden codes. He found the phrase "World Trade Center" crossing the date "September 11, 2001." Just abutting the date he discovered the word "president," and just adjacent to that he unearthed the name "George Bush." To add to the chilling impact of this find, guess what passage of Scripture President Bush quoted at the national prayer breakfast just hours after the disaster?

You guessed it. Psalm 23:4, the very verse in which these words and phrases are encoded! The verse reads, "Yea, though I walk through the valley of the shadow of death, I will fear no evil: for thou art with me; thy rod and thy staff they comfort me."

Larry found a second cluster of codes pertaining to the September 11 attack, this time in Malachi 2:10. He found "George Bush" again on the same line as "president." Other encoded words radiating from this same verse include "firemen," "airplane," "war," "knife." Even the surface text of Malachi 2:10 speaks passionately to the root of the problem that resulted in a death toll of thousands. Here is what the verse says: "Have we not all one father? hath not one God created us? Why do we deal treacherously one man against his brother, by profaning the covenant of our fathers?"

Recently, Larry found several other relevant codes in Malachi 4: 2. In this verse he found "anthrax," (twice in the same cluster), and

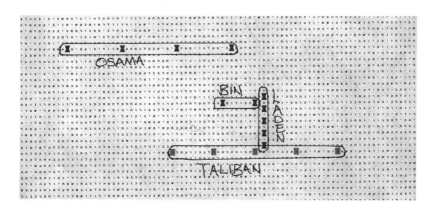

in another cluster nearby, he found "Osama," "Bin," "Laden," and "Taliban."

But perhaps the greatest significance of this finding is the message that we can glean from the surface text of Malachi 4:2. As frightening as bioterrorism and the agenda of the Taliban can seem, this verse speaks healing and comfort to those of us who call upon His name. Here is the beautiful message that Malachi 4:2 communicates to us: "But unto you that fear my name shall the Sun of righteousness arise with healing in his wings; and ye shall go forth, and grow up as calves in the stall." Calves in the stall. What an image of prosperity and protection given to us from a God who shelters us with healing wings.

"The Earth Is the Lord's"

I can't for a moment deny that Satan tempts and meddles and brings chaos and destruction and even death. But there's good news and it is this: Satan is on a short leash, folks, and the Almighty God—the Alpha and Omega, the Creator of the Universe, the Divine Lover of our souls—remains in control of all that was, all that is, and all that is to come.

Thousands of years ago, King David wrote the following words: "The earth *is* the Lord's, and the fullness thereof; the world, and they that dwell therein" (Psalm 24:1).

Indeed, I believe there is one Bible code that speaks more eloquently than any other when it comes to confirming this profound truth that David wrote about so many years ago.

As you know, everything we can touch, see, feel or taste on earth and in the universe is made up of "matter." Matter exists primarily in three different forms: gas, liquid or solid. Regardless of which form it's in, matter is made up of chemical building blocks called "elements." Surprisingly, most living things and nonliving things are made up of various combinations of only six elements: carbon, hydrogen, nitrogen, oxygen, phosphorus and sulfur.

There are, however, not just six elements, but more than a hundred. Or at least this is what scientists have discovered so far. There may well be more—in 1869, when Russian chemist Dmitri Mendeleev came up with a way of organizing the elements in a table he called "the periodic chart of elements," scientists knew about the existence of 63 different elements. Today we have discovered 109!

When Larry Mitcham programmed his computer to search for any Bible codes having to do with two of the elements—hydrogen and oxygen—he stumbled onto a mind-boggling discovery!

In a single passage of Scripture in the Old Testament book of Deuteronomy, Larry discovered a tight cluster of Bible codes containing the encrypted names of more than ninety percent of all the currently known elements. The names of these elements were unknown three thousand years ago. Many were not known or named until ten years ago. And yet several thousand years ago, they were coded in a tight cluster in the book of Deuteronomy.

Imagine! Eighty-five of the one hundred and nine chemical building blocks that make up every living and nonliving thing in the entire universe encoded in a small area of text! Are the remaining thirteen elements also there, waiting to be discovered? Larry believes they are. He continues to search for these elements, uncertain of the Hebrew spellings, but confident that he will eventually find them all encoded there.

What makes this discovery even more astounding is the fact that, in a circle surrounding this cluster of elements, the name "Elohim" has been encoded nine times. "Elohim" is a Hebrew word for *God* that is frequently used throughout the Old Testament.

Finally, let me share with you one more fascinating aspect of this particular Bible code: The verse over which many of these elements fall is none other than Deuteronomy 4:32. Let me quote that verse for you now: "For ask now of the days that are past, which were before thee, since the day that God created man upon the earth, and ask from the one side of heaven unto the other, whether there hath been any such thing as this great thing is, or hath been heard like it?"

Virtually every known chemical element that makes up the whole of creation encircled and embraced by the name of God, and encoded over a passage of Scripture marveling at the greatness of God's creation!

I don't know about you, but I find myself asking the same question that Moses asked in the fourth chapter of Deuteronomy: Have you ever heard of anything this amazing or, in fact, anything like it at all?

Our God is awesome indeed!

"O the depth of the riches both of the wisdom and knowledge of God! how unsearchable are his judgments, and his ways past finding out!" (Romans 11:33).

What secrets will be unveiled by the Bible codes that we will undoubtedly uncover tomorrow, and the next day, and the next? We have learned much about our future from the study of codes that have already been discovered, as well as from the book of Revelation, yet so much remains unknown.

Still, there is something we *do* know. It is a truth so profound it is simple. A truth analyzed by wise men yet accessible to the smallest child. A truth expounded on throughout Scripture, yet celebrated in the simplest of choruses we teach our little ones in Sunday School. And it is this: "Jesus loves me, this I know, for the Bible tells me so."

Jesus loves *you*, friend or foe, this I know. No matter what you take with you from the pages of this book, take this simple truth to heart. You are loved passionately by a perfect God who is not only the Creator of the Universe but the Architect of the future—the future of the world, and your personal future as well. You and I are in His hands, and there is simply no better—or safer—place to be if you know Him.

Bibliography

Drosnin, Michael. *The Bible Code.* New York: Simon & Schuster, 1997.

Jeffrey, Grant. *The Handwriting of God.* Toronto, Ont.: Frontier Research Publications, 1997.

LaHaye, Tim. *Revelation Unveiled.* Grand Rapids, MI: Zondervan Publishing House, 1999.

Rambsel, Yacov. *The Genesis Factor; The Amazing Mysteries of the Bible Codes.* Beverly Hills, CA: Lions Head Publishing, 2000.

Satinover, Jeffrey. *Cracking the Bible Code.* New York: Morrow, 1997.

Noah, Joseph. *Future Prospects of the World According to the Bible Code.* Boca Raton, FL: New Paradigm Books, 2002.

Missler, Chuck. *Cosmic Codes: Hidden Messages from the Edge of Eternity.* Coeur d'Alene, ID: Koinonia House, 1999.

Carl Baugh, "Creation in the Twenty-first Century" television program, Trinity Broadcasting Network.